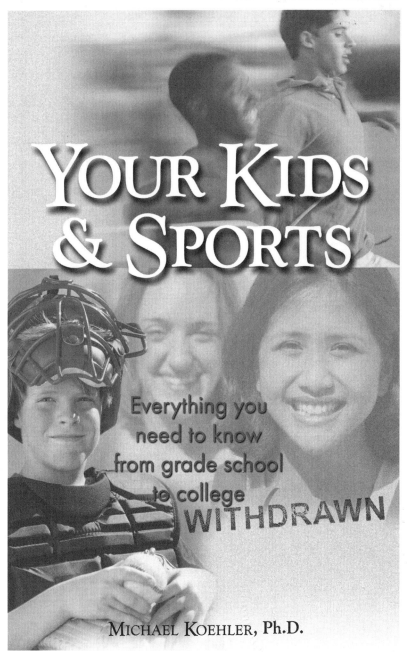

YOUR KIDS & SPORTS

Everything you
need to know
from grade school
to college

MICHAEL KOEHLER, Ph.D.

 SORIN BOOKS™ Notre Dame, Indiana

© 2004 by Michael Koehler

www.avemariapress.com

International Standard Book Number: 1-893732-72-X

Cover and text design by David R. Scholtes

Printed and bound in the United States of America.

Library of Congress Cataloging-in-Publication Data

Koehler, Mike, 1938-

  Your kids and sports : Everything you need to know from grade school to college / Michael Koehler.

    p. cm.

  ISBN 1-893732-72-X (pbk.)

  1. Sports for children. 2. Parent and child. I. Title.

GV709.2 .K64 2004

796'.083--dc22

                                          2003021926

To Coach George Kelly
—for his profound influence on me.

To my wife Pat
—for her wonderfully unconditional love.

To my daughters,
Kathleen, Carrie, and Peggy
—for sharing my love of sports.

And to my grandchildren,
Eric, Cassie, and Michael
—for keeping everyone's dreams alive.

CONTENTS

INTRODUCTION

Raising kids in today's society is not for the faint of heart. In fact, raising children has never been easy, but it is especially difficult today when so much seems to be conspiring against us. Rap music glorifies violence and defiles women; pop music and movies glamorize sex. Television talk shows and soap operas redefine "normal" behavior. Parents are being let down by some of our society's most cherished institutions. Some schools are breeding grounds for senseless violence. Some priests are abusing children. Some teachers are having babies with their students.

Looking to sports for principled behavior doesn't help much either. There have been reports of some coaches in youth programs sexually abusing their athletes. Social anomalies like Dennis Rodman and Mike Tyson have become poster boys for media moguls who capitalize on the "role muddles" they create for millions of young people. Of course, one could argue that professional athletes have always behaved outlandishly. Ty Cobb climbed into the bleachers more than once to silence hecklers, and Jim Thorpe and his teammates were often frisked for guns and knives before being allowed to get off trains in the early days of the NFL.

Many of us still honor and respect most of our athletic institutions, but we now must study them a little more carefully than we once did. Like Teddy Roosevelt who "walked softly but carried a big stick," you and I now must "trust freely but keep an open eye." Unfortunately, we need to keep this open eye not only to bad behavior in our schools,

YOUR KIDS AND SPORTS

churches, and sports arenas but also to lack of character. A feeling of self-indulgence has taken over much of our society. "What I *have*" is now often more important than "What I *am*," and winning is a whole lot more important than making the effort to win. In some schools and homes, winning is so important that lying and cheating have become quasi-acceptable ways of achieving it.

Still, many of us are trying valiantly to be Bill Cosby parents despite living in an Ozzy Osbourne world. Family values and moral codes are constant issues in our homes and schools. As a result we want a little help leading our children along the confusing and often directionless path that leads to a happy and healthy adulthood for them. For many reasons the path is getting bumpy, rutted, and full of twists and turns.

In our desire for our kids to be good as well as successful, we look to coaches and sports programs to help them travel the path. But something's happening out there that's not only causing kids to quit sports programs, but causing conscientious parents to question the value of all forms of athletic competition for their children. Competition has become fierce and unpleasant. Little League, Pop Warner, Pee Wee, and junior high programs introduce young children to levels of stress—from parents as well as coaches—that rival even the most competitive high school and college programs.

Sports are disappointing lots of kids. How do we turn the tide? If you want a sports experience to be everything it can be for your child, you probably need some help. This book provides it. It provides information, stories, advice, even slogans that give direction to parents who want athletic competition to fulfill its promises to youngsters. This book offers the specifics on what to ask and what to look for in athletic programs at every level: youth programs to secondary school activities. It also offers advice on how to look for it.

Chapter One discusses the purposes of athletic competition and the learning experiences kids can gain from both winning and losing. It distinguishes between wanting to win and needing to win and identifies the characteristics of a good coach and a good program.

Chapter Two explores the parent's role and looks at such specifics as choosing the right sport, understanding a little about the sport, maintaining good communication with kids and coaches, and avoiding the pitfalls of over-identifying or under-identifying with your child's accomplishments.

Chapter Three considers the conditioning needs of young athletes. It identifies several myths about weight lifting and nutrition and discusses the child's growth and development in relation to vigorous strength and aerobic training.

Chapter Four addresses the issue of injury and the young athlete. It details the difference between pain and fatigue, addresses several causes of injury, and offers ways to encourage and support injured athletes. Most importantly, it identifies the appropriate time for young athletes to return to competition after an injury.

Chapter Five explores the very real issue of young athletes and burnout. It discusses why kids burn out and how to avoid it by ensuring that their participation is positive, relatively stress-free, and, above all, fun. Children are quitting organized sports at earlier and earlier ages. It's important that parents understand why and are in a position to do something about it.

Chapter Six looks at the real world of athletic scholarships by emphasizing the importance of academics, explaining the kinds of courses athletes should take in school, looking at the actual availability of scholarships, and, if warranted, identifying processes for getting scholarships.

Chapter Seven examines the statistics and warning signs of drug use. It considers all drugs, including tobacco, alcohol, and steroids. It transforms most parents' fear and confusion into an understanding of the kinds of drugs and their varying effects on kids. Parents who understand the warning signs of drug use are in a better position than other parents not only to intervene, but to actually stop their children from using. When kids know that *you* know and when you can share with them the realities of drug use, they are more likely not to risk what you both suddenly understand to be the dangers of drug use.

Chapter Eight provides stories about young athletes that illustrate the positives and negatives of athletic participation for young and old alike. It also quotes prominent sports figures and serves as a dramatic and revealing summary of the book. Some of these stories demonstrate that athletic competition is not all that it's cracked up to be, but, perhaps more importantly, they reaffirm the value of what sports *can* be—one of the most profound and enjoyable experiences in your child's life. You can help guarantee such an experience when you know everything you need to know about the purposes of athletics, the signs of good coaching, even important insights into nutrition, burnout, strength training, aerobics, and drug use. This book will help you and your children find and shape athletic programs that provide the fun and build the character kids need to be successful and happy in life.

1.
WHAT DO PARENTS WANT FOR THEIR KIDS?

Did You Know?

- Of the twenty million children who participate in sports programs every year, 70 percent stop by the age of thirteen.

- Most preteens quit sports because they are no longer having fun.

- The kids themselves report that sports are too competitive.

It's no startling revelation to say that most parents want sports for their kids. Kids need the social, physical, and emotional benefits of healthy competition and team membership, and they need relationships with adults who care about them and encourage their self-discipline and commitment. The array of athletic activities available in most communities usually offers all these things. So why are the above statistics so relevant, and what do they suggest for most parents?

They are disturbing facts, especially to a guy like me who has devoted much of his life to working with kids. Games to me have always seemed synonymous with kids. In fact, I've always believed that games are what kids do best. For most children, games are probably the best way to promote their healthy growth. From peek-a-boo, catch, and flash cards, to fast balls and quick openers, games teach kids important skills in life—not just in sports.

So what's happening out there? Why are kids abandoning an experience that promises so much? Probably because it's not delivering. Winning has become too important to adults and, now, to many kids. Many coaches and, let's admit it, parents have organized the fun right out of sports. Unfortunately, competition is getting all the blame. It's become a bad word to most fair-minded parents. So let's start this chapter by taking a closer look at it.

What is competition? Sports competition is all about winning and losing. If it weren't, we wouldn't keep score. Every competitor, no matter how young or old, tries to win the game, to win the race, even to win a place on the team. Youngsters may want fun and parents may want growth experiences for their kids, but the reason athletes walk onto the field or the court is to win. The early Greeks may have valued amateurism in the ancient Olympics, but they sought victory as vigorously as today's toughest competitor.

There's nothing wrong with that. Winning and losing are accepted facts in sports. No one wants to eliminate scoring; folks just want to score more than the other guy. Crowds tear down goal posts after a big win—never the scoreboard. Parents should realize, therefore, that there's nothing wrong with trying to win. We must also realize that there's a lot to be learned from winning—and losing. First of all, however, we must understand that winning and losing have different meanings at different levels of competition.

Emphasize the differences between the pros and the Pee Wees. The exclusive focus of professional sports is to make a buck—a lot of bucks. Pee Wee sports, Little League, Pop Warner, and junior high and secondary school programs need money only to get off the ground. Once organized and funded, their exclusive focus is on the development of kids—at least it should be.

When we seek a sports program for our kids, therefore, we want one that puts the needs of the kids ahead of any thought of winning or losing, certainly of money. So what do you look for in a good sports program for kids? You look for exactly the same things Michigan State University discovered when they asked kids what they wanted from athletic participation:

1. to have fun,

2. to improve and learn skills,

3. to join friends and make new friends,

4. to get excited,

5. to be successful,

6. to get physically fit.

Fun. Kids want to have fun. These goals don't differ much from what most parents want for their kids. Parents want even more. But you and I also go several steps further. We have a strong sense of what our kids need in life to be successful and happy, so we also want our kids to:

- be physically fit and to improve their performance,

- learn leadership and respect for authority,

- enjoy purposeful and healthy competition,

- learn to cooperate,

- develop self-esteem and self-confidence,

- assume responsibility,

- experience the values of hard work,

- think positively,

- enjoy a sense of belonging,

- associate with positive role models,

- value performance over outcome.

Let's admit it. Most parents really haven't given much thought to these aspects of sports competition. I wouldn't have given them much thought either if I hadn't been fortunate enough to bump into a few outstanding coaches during my playing and coaching days. Folks like George Kelly of the University of Notre Dame (he coached me at Marquette University and, later, at Nebraska) taught me what we also want kids to learn to:

- release tension,

- learn to control anger,

- be self-critical,

- reflect on all aspects of their behavior,

- accept failure as a learning experience,

- accept victory with humility, defeat with dignity,

- develop self-discipline,

- make commitments,

- strive for consistency in everything they do,

- understand that effort is more important than winning,

- develop integrity,

- improve the ability to focus,

- learn to take themselves less seriously.

This list suggests the scope of what sports can do to develop character and self-discipline in kids. It's also obvious that these purposes fly in the face of much of what we see and hear in the media. They are on the flip side of the strutting, trash-talking, chest-bumping foolishness we see in professional and some college sports, and they identify levels of self-discipline that are completely foreign to the self-indulgent and often violent behaviors of some professional athletes.

The purposes are an important starting point. Parents want to guarantee these purposes by feeling confident that all the adults involved in the program want to do everything in their power to assure the same purposes. The purposes identify what needs to be accomplished for kids. Next most important is how to accomplish them. In essence, we want all coaches, parents, and athletes to work toward these purposes, not subvert them by over-emphasizing winning, failing to relate to each other, or spouting some short-sighted view of competition.

We all have to be on the same page. Good youth programs and junior high and secondary programs can provide all these purposes. But the coaches and people who are responsible for the organization of the program must be on the same page we are. If their focus is exclusively on winning, maybe to the point of abusing kids, we want to avoid the program—or seek to change it. Unfortunately, there are too many programs like that out there. That's why more than half the youngsters who get involved in organized sports quit before their teens.

Michigan State's Youth Sports Institute also revealed the two top reasons kids quit sports: "I was no longer interested" and "It was no longer fun." This is disturbing news for parents who look to coaches and other professionals for help raising their kids.

Seven Questions Parents Need to Ask About a Program

So what do we do when looking for a program for our kids? Ask these seven questions while you're looking:

1. When you attend meetings, does the coach lecture to you or does (s)he engage you in discussion?

2. Are you encouraged to ask questions?

3. Does the coach make you feel that you and other parents are an integral part of the program?

4. Does the coach explain his or her experiences and special training as a coach?

5. Are you invited to attend practices?

6. Are you invited to suggest or affirm the objectives of the program?

7. Does the coach express a positive approach to coaching or is (s)he a frustrated ex-athlete who hopes to find competitive satisfaction in driving kids relentlessly?

Listen carefully to the coach during meetings for answers to these questions, even ask him or her for responses. Then look for hints of the coach's priorities in such specifics as his or her attention to:

- Necessary equipment: Is it on hand or do you have to purchase it? Regardless of availability, make sure the child has it, and make sure it fits properly.

- Practice schedules: Do they accommodate fundamental skills, water breaks, and rest time?

- The length of practices and contests: Are they reasonable, or do they interfere with family priorities and the child's study needs?

- Team rules and consequences: Are the rules fair and enforceable? Are the consequences reasonable?

- Events during the season: Has the coach scheduled occasions for athletes, coaches, and parents to socialize and to develop among everyone a sense of "family"?

Seven Questions Before Choosing a Sports Camp

These questions are equally appropriate for parents who are choosing among a variety of sports camps that are available every summer. Whether a youth camp or a program designed for preteens and teens, you want the camp to do fundamentally the same things. You want your child to have fun, to keep busy, to make friends, and to learn about his or her sport. But more, you want it to be a total learning experience, a chance for your child not only to develop athletic skills, but to learn about winning and losing and to develop character. And, above all, you want your child to be safe. So ask these questions before choosing a program:

1. What are the motivations of the people who have organized the program? Are they out just to make a buck, or have they developed a track record of caring about kids? *Remember:* Read the brochure carefully and be sure to ask questions. Call if necessary to get your questions answered.

2. What condition is the equipment in? High quality, well-fitting equipment is essential if kids are to practice and compete safely. *Remember:* Kids are being injured, even dying, unnecessarily every year across the country because of poor coaching and faulty equipment. Don't fear being pushy. Check it out.

3. Is the focus exclusively on winning? Is that all the brochure or representatives of the program talks about? *Remember:* The proper focus for kids, especially at sports camps, is on performance—not outcome.

4. Do the activities focus primarily on team competitions, or do they provide one-on-one instruction and drill time? *Remember:* Most programs that focus primarily on team competitions are more interested in

identifying and possibly recruiting college athletes than helping young athletes to develop their skills.

5. Do the coaches and program coordinators brag about their emphasis on character and positive values, or is their emphasis exclusively on skill development? More importantly, do they actually do what they say they will do? *Remember:* Good coaches understand the importance of character in all forms of competition—athletic or otherwise—and they teach it every chance they get.

6. Who will be doing the actual coaching, student athletes or advertised coaches? *Remember:* Some camps may be sponsored by big-name coaches from major universities, but many of them show up just to introduce themselves and welcome the kids to the camp, then they head for the nearest walleye hole.

7. What, then, are the qualifications of the people who will be doing the actual coaching? *Remember:* If the coaches are not properly qualified, kids may not only receive incorrect information, but also be subject to unnecessary injury.

A young friend of mine in Wisconsin went every year to a camp run by an outstanding quarterback coach, Jeff Trickey, who impressed the kids more by his emphasis on character than by his knowledge of quarterback technique, and he was one of the best in the nation when it came to teaching technique. My friend remembers the first time he sat before Trickey after a practice. Jeff told all the athletes that they had one homework assignment that evening, something they absolutely had to do before the next day's practice: "Go home tonight and give your mom and dad a big hug. They are the most important people in your life. Let them know it."

The Five Characteristics of a Good Coach

A good coach understands that character and fundamental skills are an unbeatable combination. What else must parents look for in a coach? How do good coaches accommodate all the needs of kids? What do you look for in the philosophy of your child's coach? Good coaches—at any level of competition—display five essential characteristics mentioned earlier in this section and establish a coaching philosophy that helps their athletes:

Emphasize performance over outcome. This characteristic is critical. Good coaches don't want kids to worry about winning or losing. They want them only to focus on the immediate performance of their skills and to make a total effort, in essence to live in the moment. You have good reason to be concerned, therefore, if your child's coach talks only about developing a winning program. As a matter of fact, you have reason to be concerned about your own motives if you share that goal.

Think positively. The coach who emphasizes positive relationships and positive thinking energizes and empowers kids. (S)he reduces stress and shows them how to relax, not just during athletic competition, but throughout the day. Coaches who are negative restrict kids, create stress, and ultimately provoke behaviors among athletes that are failure-oriented.

Maintain a narrow focus. To be successful at anything, kids must learn to focus on the moment, to live in the here and now. Whether they're shooting a free throw, catching a baseball, or completing a homework assignment, they must give their complete attention to the task. Good coaches teach this by providing good-natured but frequent reminders to kids, not by yelling at them. Yelling is a negative behavior, failure-oriented because it actually interferes with the child's focus.

Be competent and self-confident. One thing I'm certain of is that most of us can do anything—anything—if we put our minds to it and believe we can do it. I've seen young athletes perform well beyond their talent levels simply because they believed they could. And they believed they could because they knew that their parents and coaches believed they could. Such behavior is the essence of a self-fulfilling prophecy. We know that if we genuinely believe in our kids and give them the necessary instruction and the help they need, they can accomplish most anything. This may be the most important thing a good coach does.

Have character. I learned early in my coaching career that winners win and losers lose. Winners win at everything they do, just as losers always manage to fall short of the mark, no matter what that mark is. The difference between the two is character. Good coaches realize this by emphasizing character-building with their kids and by modeling good character on and off the field. Like good parents, good coaches understand that kids will never do anything special in life until they *are* something special.

Character: Develop One, Don't Be One

Any good program helps kids become something special. Good coaches regard character as a tool that youngsters use to *be* special and to *do* special things. They also recognize that the most special thing young athletes *do* is make a maximum effort. My most special accomplishment is not the defeat of an opponent, but the mastery of myself. Kids will earn their share of victories once they learn this kind of self-discipline and commitment, the kind of commitment that promotes a focused, maximum effort.

More to look for in a good coach. Good coaches don't tolerate misbehavior. They prohibit swearing, taunting opponents, laughing at opponent's mistakes, or jeering from the sidelines. They demand classy behavior, things like:

- shaking hands at the end of a contest or event,

- taking time to talk with opponents,

- congratulating outstanding opponents for their performance,

- making a presentable appearance before and after the contest,

- acting maturely and responsibly after a victory,

- holding their heads high after a loss.

Learning experiences in sports are everywhere. If coaches don't require such behaviors from kids, the kids miss out on a variety of valuable learning experiences. Much can be learned from winning, but even more from losing. The lessons may be more severe and harder to swallow, but they last longer and make a greater impact. If losses are only occasional, it's easier to get back on track. But when losing becomes habitual, coaches and parents have their work cut out for them. Keep these suggestions in mind when your child loses—at anything, and check to see if your child's coach is doing the same things.

First look at your own behavior. Look in the nearest mirror to see if you're putting on too much heat or doing something else wrong. If you are—stop. If you want to be a good model to your children, you must have the courage to change your behavior, too. The same is true of your child's coach.

After you've looked at yourself and your child's coach, identify the problem. This means talking to the child—maybe to the coach. Be careful not to focus just on symptoms. Doctors know that a focus only on symptoms obscures the real problem—and the patient sometimes dies. You don't want your child's enthusiasm for sports to die, so take the time to find the real problem.

The child may seem unmotivated or in a rut and keep making the same mistakes. The problem may not be lack of motivation, it may be problems with fundamental skills or confusion about assignments.

This can be true about classwork, too. The apparent unwillingness to do necessary work can involve a whole lot more than resistance. Find the real problem.

Next, find the most appropriate solutions, remembering that the best solutions may involve changes in *you* or the *coach*. When applying solutions, remember this coaching maxim: Hug a loser and push a winner. Winners have the confidence to respond positively to a good, hard push. Losers don't. Put your arm around the child who loses and do your best to rebuild his or her sagging confidence. Remember poet John Dryden's quote: "For they win who believe they can." So expect a lot from kids, but, for the child who loses, push less and praise a whole lot more.

Most important, recognize that, like winning, losing can become a habit. Habits are chains. At first, they're too weak to be felt; later, too strong to be broken. Don't let the chain of losing get strong. Keep emphasizing the difference between losing and failing. Losers keep trying; failures quit. When kids don't quit, winning is inevitable.

Failure: A Chance to Grow, Never an Excuse to Fail

Persistence is its own reward. As Vince Lombardi said years ago, the will to win is the most important thing in sports. Any good coach realizes that the outcome of the game is significantly less important than the effort kids put into winning it. I learned many years ago as a player and coach that the harder I worked, the luckier I got. This is a valuable lesson for children.

Remember the story of the Scotsman who was leaving home to fight for his independence? His son asked him: "Dad, what are you doing? You can't possibly win." I'll never forget his answer. "I'm not going there to win—I'm going there to *fight*!" That's what we want our kids to learn from sports, to make a maximum effort in spite of the outcome. We want them to keep trying, to keep fighting. It may not produce a string of victories, but it will result in a whole lot of character. With character, victory is just around the corner.

The Difference Between Wanting to Win and Needing to Win

This suggests a very important point for the parents of young athletes. Each of us must understand that kids with character and self-discipline *want* to win. In the minds of most good coaches, they have "the *will* to win." It is this will to win that gives them the strength to work hard and to persist in their efforts. Athletes with strong wills also have strong "won'ts." They won't back off a total effort. They won't concentrate on their own needs and disregard the team's purposes. They won't use drugs. They won't daydream or fail to focus on peak performance. They won't just lie there when they get knocked down.

The will to win is not the same as the need to win. Kids who *need* to *win* will focus on their own needs or use drugs to enhance their performance. They are more likely than other kids to cheat because their goal is to satisfy their need to win—at all costs. Their goal is not character. We have all learned that kids, any of us for that matter, will do whatever is necessary to satisfy an all-consuming need. Kids who desperately need food will risk their safety to get it.

Kids who need safety will join gangs to find it. And when things get tough, they'll be the first to back off a total effort, the first to just lie there when they get knocked down.

A need to win can cause the wrong behaviors. People with all-consuming needs are unable to ignore them. The stronger the needs become, the harder kids will try to satisfy them. When the need becomes that pronounced, someone other than the child may be to blame. Pushy parents and pushy coaches can do a world of harm to kids.

Keep things in perspective. The difference between wanting to win and needing to win is formidable. Our job as parents is to keep it in perspective. When we emphasize performance over outcome and effort over victory, we do much to maintain our perspective. And I won't spout silliness like: "A billion Chinese don't give a hoot in Hades about the outcome of a particular game." I know China may not care about it, but your child does. I hated to lose, but I also realized—and I made sure that my kids did, too—that a loss involved disappointment, not despair.

Three Ways to Help Kids Avoid the Need to Win

Maintain perspective. You and your child may focus on one particular goal, such as winning a game or getting an A, but it's important to recognize that failure to realize the goal is not the end of the world. Usually, it's just a matter of establishing a better goal. If the goal is to perform to the best of your ability instead of merely winning the game, to study as hard as you can instead of focusing on an A, the specific outcome is less important. That's why it's so important for young athletes—all of us, for that matter—to emphasize performance over outcome. "Study hard; the grade will take care of itself." "Practice hard; the game will take care of itself."

Focus on the right things. Help develop your child's self-concept based on the good he or she does rather than the reward. If helping others, cooperating with teammates, making a maximum effort, or taking some cookies to an elderly neighbor are his or her standards for success, every child in this country, even the most intellectually or athletically challenged, can develop a positive self-concept. Think about this: What does our country need more, kids with straight-A averages and all-conference honors or children who persevere and have a generous, loving spirit?

Reassess your own wants and needs. The media are full of role "muddles," fictitious and real-life folks who spout "Me first" every time they open their mouths. It is especially important, therefore, that you and I model the right kinds of behaviors for our kids. Society's best role models are sitting in the same room with their children almost every night.

Let's Wrap It Up

Good parents are the first to recognize the danger of athletic competition for something other than its own sake. If youngsters compete athletically to get awards and honors, all-conference recognition, college scholarships, or because of a burning need to win, they are involved in sports for the wrong reasons. And it's our job to straighten them out. Kids have to focus on performance if they are to gain anything from athletic competition.

We must instill this sense of character in our children. Character is essential when the competition gets stiff, when self-focus must give way to cooperation. Character is running so hard that you're convinced you can't take another step—but you do. It's thinking you can't lift yourself off the ground again—but you do. Jack Dempsey's quote comes to mind: "Champions are people who get up—when they can't." We want our kids to have such character. We want them to focus on the here and now and on the performance that leads to the kinds of outcomes that are consistent with our values.

Only when our children dedicate themselves to hard work, self-sacrifice, mutual cooperation, the mastery of their assignments and skills, and the realization of individual and team goals do they become winners. Such dedication requires self-discipline. Without it, children rarely make commitments or develop the consistency that leads to the successful performance of their skills. Take the time to find athletic programs and coaches that share your feelings about these issues.

2.
THE PARENT'S ROLE

Did You Know?

- At the end of a recent youth football game in Pennsylvania, police were called to stop a brawl involving at least fifty parents and kids.

- A dad in the Midwest was found guilty of solicitation to commit simple assault for giving a Little League pitcher two dollars to hit an opposing batter.

- A father in a major Southwestern metropolitan area got two days in jail for sharpening his son's football helmet buckle. It cut five opposing players.

- A dad in Florida was charged with aggravated battery when he broke an umpire's jaw while being ejected from a game.

I had an experience that was equally troubling. During a recent meeting with my family doctor, I discussed this book. A former football player with more than his share of joint problems, he thought it was a great idea and agreed that it was needed by parents, students, and fans alike. He was particularly interested in the parents perspective because he had just met a parent who wanted him to prescribe human growth hormone for her son.

Shocked, I asked him, "Are you saying that the boy's *mother* wanted the prescription?" He nodded and said that her son wasn't tall enough for college recruiters. He then indicated that her request was not unusual; that he receives similar requests regularly, maybe not for human growth hormone but for performance enhancers and pain killers. He said that it was about time someone took a careful look at this issue. "The fantasy of a scholarship is so important to this mother," he said, "that she's willing to risk her son's health to get it."

Isn't it amazing how many of us would rather be destroyed by our own fantasies than saved by someone else's truth? Well, here's another truth. My doctor also indicated that, as determined by a study in Iowa, a significant percentage of high school football players already have traumatic arthritis. They will suffer from it for the rest of their lives—just as I do. I played fullback and outside linebacker for Marquette University and the University of Nebraska and do more than my share of grimacing and grunting every time I get out of my chair.

Fortunately, my daughter Carrie is unaffected by the fantasy side of football, in spite of the fact that her husband, her dad, her grandfather, and her great-grandfather (Jim Thorpe) all played the game. Listening to me get out of my chair and bend over to tie my shoes convinced her that my grandson would never play the game. He is now focusing on basketball and baseball.

She got a recent jolt, however, when she overheard a comment from her younger sister who played basketball for Tulsa University. Peggy was getting up from the dinner table when she gave a grunt and remarked immediately, "Oh no, I'm making my father's noise!"

Sometimes fathers—and mothers—make a kind of noise that can be a whole lot worse. As reported in *Sports Illustrated* in July of 2000, Fred Engh, the president of the National Alliance for Youth Sports, asserted that in 1995, one might expect 5 percent of parents to make spectacles of themselves at the athletic contests of their children. Only five years later, that number rose to 15 percent. Said Engh, "It borders on insanity. Every year I see more and more ugly things."

Wrote an umpire recently about youth sports: "I had to throw both coaches out of a game for foul language. One was our police chief, the other our mayor."

Even when not using abusive language or engaging in violence, too many parents have transformed the cheering section into the jeering section. Fortunately, we're not talking about the majority of parents, but even 15 percent can foul the air with abusive comments and ruin an otherwise wholesome experience for everyone, especially their children, who usually want to have nothing more than a good time.

Said a young Midwestern athlete: "We have the 'Heckling Crew.' They get shirts every year and put nicknames on the back. There were like 100 shirts printed this year."

The Purposes of Sport

Many parents today not only watch sporting spectacles, they are sporting spectacles. They simply don't understand what youth sports are all about. Many are more interested in satisfying their own misguided need for recognition than helping their children enjoy their athletic experiences and learn from them.

The purposes and advantages of sports competition for kids are apparent to many of us, but consider these additional statistics for girls in school. They come from The Women's Sports Federation:

- Girls who play sports are 92 percent less likely to use drugs.

- They are 80 percent less likely to get pregnant while still in school.

- They are three times more likely to graduate from high school.

In spite of such obvious advantages, youngsters still quit sports, primarily because of the abuses they find. Insults from fans, rebukes from coaches, even demands from their parents transform a game into a grind. Let's face it, when parents become fans, opposing players become "the enemy," and coaches become drill sergeants, the thrill of competition doesn't last long. And some of us wonder why kids quit sports and fail to realize the many advantages of participation. Such problems can be avoided by a little diligence on our part. All we need is an understanding of why and how kids get involved in sports and what we want for them.

> *A star player for a Chicago-area girls basketball team reported recently in the media: "Going into the locker room at halftime, I got spit on five times by opposing fans."*

Four Steps to Motivate Your Child

Why we want our kids involved in sports is obvious. Certainly, one of our primary reasons is that we know instinctively what the research confirms: Kids involved in sports are more successful in school and later in life. The claim is supported by countless university studies. My experience indicates that it's true, even in some of the most misunderstood sports programs.

> *Knowing that I played for the University of Nebraska, a couple of my friends like to tease me with the question: "What does the N on the Nebraska helmet stand for?" I ask, "What?" and they gleefully shout, "Knowledge!"*

It's always intrigued me that the University of Nebraska has more Academic All-Americans than any other school in the nation, including Harvard and Yale. Most folks don't know this. All those media claims and the occasional inarticulate mumblings of a few professional athletes to the contrary, most junior high school, secondary, and college athletes are successful in school, even in the most successful athletic programs. Many parents sense this and want their kids to be involved in such activities. How we get them involved is the key.

1. *Let the Child Choose the Sport*

Most kids already are interested in one or more sports, and, if undecided, they are willing to experiment until they find the one or two they most enjoy. But most important is their right to choose or *not to choose* the sport they want. So the first "must" for parents is to help their kids decide by:

- providing information,
- being willing listeners,
- asking good questions,
- being supportive.

Not by:
- coercing,
- intimidating,
- pushing,
- bribing,
- pressuring.

Any decision to play a sport must be the child's. One of the first things we learn as parents is that kids commit readily to what *they* want. They sometimes have problems, even resist, the things *we* want for them. Yes, yes, I know. Our motives are noble, and our approach is usually flawless. But that doesn't change the fact that if I make the decision, *I* own it. If you make the decision, *you* own it. It's that simple.

So why do most kids choose certain sports? To have fun—nothing more, nothing less. That's the inalienable right of all of us. They don't need thousands of adoring fans, just the one or two they find at home. So recognize what they hope to find in sports, then help them find it.

2. *Help the Child Choose the Best Level of Competition*

The level of competition has a lot to do with the amount of fun they'll find. If the coach pushes too hard, the pressure from the stands to win is too evident, or teammates or opponents are too big, the experience is likely to provide more stress than fun. For really young or slowly developing youngsters, contact sports are a bad choice. When the child's skeleton isn't fully formed, joint injury is more possible and a future of traumatic arthritis is more likely.

Watching a Pop Warner game with a friend a few years ago, I heard a coach berate a young player by actually screaming, "What do you think this is—a game?!"

Coaches and parents must recognize that Little League and Pop Warner playing fields are not training grounds for future professionals. They should be enjoyable and relatively stress-free learning experiences that are developmentally appropriate for all kids. If the coach or anyone associated with the program fails to realize this, help the child find another sport or activity, no matter how many of his or her friends are joining up.

What about traveling teams? Well, there's some good news and some bad news about traveling teams. The good news is that being selected to a traveling team is high praise for most kids. It's a compliment to their abilities and an opportunity to compete against the best athletes at their age levels. It sets the stage for selected young athletes to refine their skills and to establish themselves as promising prospects for future levels of competition.

Therein lies some of the bad news. Many of these children are "promising" for no other reason than they are bigger and stronger than other kids in their age groups. As a result, they perform better. Coaches, parents, and the athletes themselves, however, must never think of these kids as elite or gifted. Being physically precocious is not the same as being the next Michael Jordan. These kids simply got a head start in life's developmental race toward maturity.

Many of their teammates are slower out of the blocks but often catch and even pass the early starters. It's important, therefore, to keep traveling teams in perspective. If your child is selected to one, enjoy the compliment but continue to focus on the competition as fun—not as the first step toward a scholarship. If your child is rejected by one, all is not lost. The sport and all the fun it involves is still available, and, with a little added growth or maturity, the child can attain tougher levels of competition.

Sometimes we go too far. Even young, gifted athletes who have refined their skills and have legitimate futures in their sports have to guard against inappropriate competitive levels. High school basketball players—even elementary school athletes—now find themselves being invited to play in regional or national all-star national tournaments, community leagues, camps sponsored by shoe companies, and Amateur Athletic Union (AAU) championships—in addition to their regular school competitions.

In a matter of a few months, many of these kids, some of whom are only seventh- and eighth-graders, may play in as many as 100 games. As reported by Taylor Bell, sportswriter for the Chicago Sun-Times, at least one group is doing something about it. In Illinois, the Illinois Basketball Coaches Association (IBCA) is seeking to limit student involvement beyond the regular school season. Says IBCA President, Chuck Rolinski, "I saw eighth-graders and freshmen being flown all over the country for games. Then parents began asking coaches why their kids weren't playing. Then high school coaches lost control to summer coaches. We need to do something about it."

Indeed we do. You might argue that such levels of exposure are important for gifted athletes, and maybe you're right. We're talking about the potential for a lot of money, and, after all, many kids and their parents are finding heroes in sports. Why not? Nowhere else in society is perfection more demonstrable. These folks are really good, and they work hard at what they do. But let's admit it, many of them also behave in some of the strangest ways. They also manage to attract bands of beer-drinking banshees who applaud this strangeness.

We are left to conclude that even gifted athletes need time for something other than a particular sport. Our job as parents is not to encourage junior to think of himself as Tom the Basketball or Football Player but as Tom the Total Person. We want Tom to think of himself as well-rounded, intelligent, mature, considerate, and happy. Sports alone will not guarantee such a self-concept. It's up to you and me to provide the balance between the right sport and too much of the right sport.

3. Don't Overreact If the Child Chooses Not to Play

Not all kids are talented or committed to certain sports. You may have been a high school All-American and a starting fullback in college, but if junior chooses a sport other than football or no sport at all, you have a couple very important things to do. One, respect the child's choice. His reasons may be good. Discuss them with him or her. If the reasons are suspect, help the child re-evaluate them. Two, look carefully at your own behavior or the behaviors of others familiar with the family. Children pushed into following in the footsteps of others in the family can resist a sport as vigorously as you or others push it.

I entered high school carrying a load of family expectations that I would play football. My dad had played for the school, and my grandfather was Jim Thorpe. I quit just a few weeks into my sophomore year. Months later, realizing that it was now my choice, I played again. This time I learned to love the game—on my terms.

There is no doubt that genetic "gifts" are passed down from one family member to another. Athletic talent is hereditary. Love of a particular sport, however, is not. In addition, parents must keep in mind that "living up" to a successful family member is difficult for many kids. The best way to help them with such a problem—and, incidentally, the best way to get them involved in the sport—is to encourage them to consider the circumstances and to make the decision themselves.

4. *Respect the Child's Decision.*

Provide counsel but respect your child's decision. The best way to do this is to share enthusiasm for the sport by accompanying the child to meetings, attending games, and providing support and acceptance no matter what level of success the child realizes. The most important goal of athletic participation, especially at early levels, is fun. Kids quit if they don't have fun, and they choose other sports if the first experience is not everything they expected.

An important key is to keep expectations in line with experiences. If the child expects to have fun and *does* have fun, the experience was successful, and the likelihood is that he or she learned a lot, not only about the sport but about commitment, teamwork, relationships, and responsibility. You and I may call it play, but much can be learned from play. Famed child psychologist Jean Piaget said that play is the business of childhood. And the more fun it is, the more the child is likely to learn.

Understand Your Child's Sport

The better you understand your child's sport, the more you'll enjoy it and be able to share your enthusiasm for it. No one expects you to be a coaching genius. You don't have to understand the strategic effectiveness of a gap stack forty-four versus a double wing formation. But it helps to distinguish between offense and defense and to know what position your child plays.

My cousin Sharon is Jim Thorpe's granddaughter. Yet, when I asked her before one of her son's first football games what position he played, she said, "You know, I'm really not sure. I think he plays tailgate."

Finding Available Resources. You should learn the basic rules, something about the skills involved, and a little about strategy. You might even shock your child over the dinner table and earn a piece of that new-found respect kids have for moms and dads who enter their worlds. Fortunately, learning about a sport isn't hard. Your child's coach can direct you to libraries or bookstores for materials. The coach might also provide information at meetings and/or demonstrations during early practices to introduce parents to fundamentals and safety measures.

Helping the Coach Help You. All parents, especially those with little background in the sport, should attend such meetings. If the coach fails to offer such meetings or demonstrations, ask him or her to plan one or more. Offer your help by contacting parents, developing and duplicating written materials, providing snacks, or setting up the area. You will learn more, and you'll provide a valuable service for your community or school.

Don't Over-Identify or Under-Identify. Parents, some more than others, must constantly remind themselves that this is their child's sport, not theirs. We all identify with our kids and we want the best for them. Sometimes, however, we identify too strongly with them. When our children become extensions of us, they lose their personal identity. So do we. We begin to define ourselves and find our self-worth in the accomplishments of our kids.

> *A youth umpire indicated to me recently: "Some parents and coaches use children as their own last chance to be winners. How do you respond to that?"*

At one extreme, consider the frustrated athlete who loved sports but never found success. At the other, consider the high school or college stars who expect their children to follow in their footsteps. When their successes or failures as adults depend on the accomplishments of their children, the children carry a heavy load. They learn quickly that more is on the line than winning or losing a game. When the love and respect of parents is based on athletic performance, kids feel tension and lose interest in all forms of athletic activity.

The Value of Unconditional Love. When kids know that they are loved no matter how successful they are on the field or in the classroom, they develop personality strength and character. They recognize the good in themselves and understand that their worth as human beings depends more on what they *are* and less on what they *do* or what they *have*. The failure of parents to provide such love, by over-identifying or under-identifying with their children, hurts kids' self-concepts and interferes with their growth toward adulthood.

Be Honest About Your Needs: Five Important Questions

When your child decides on a sport, ask yourself these questions:

1. *Can you share your child's commitment to the sport?* You don't have to attend all the practices, but you should find the time to attend as many contests as possible and to find opportunities for the child to share fears and happy moments. Can you ask questions and listen to answers, giving support whenever possible?

2. *Can you be a good role model?* Parents with no self-control model impulsive behavior for their children. Kids are impulsive enough as it is. They need adults in their lives who model self-control and deliberate, thoughtful behavior.

3. *Can you let go of your child?* Coaches can become God figures in the lives of children. Can you share with someone else the admiration your child had exclusively for you? Can you let your child make his or her own decisions? Can you offer advice and support but leave the final decision up to the child? Can you live with the fact that sports is one of your earliest experiences with letting go?

4. *Can you deal with losing?* Can you avoid being embarrassed or ashamed when your child loses or cries after a contest? More importantly, can you see opportunities for growth and learning in each loss?

5. *Can you deal with winning?* This can be an insidious problem for parents. Some parents are unable to accept their children's successes without pointing out flaws or comparing the performance to their own when they played. Sports is a child-centered activity. We should do everything in our power to keep it that way.

Five Paths to Success

Once we control our levels of identification with our children, we are in an excellent position to help them find success. We help our children realize their potential by promoting these five paths to success:

1. *Love Yourself.* Children love themselves when they realize that other people, especially their parents, love them. This is yet another argument for unconditional love, but kids also love themselves when they know they deserve to be loved. In essence, if children want to *do* something special, whether in sports or in life, they must first *be* something special. Our job as parents is to walk this path with them, helping them discover along the way the values of hard work, commitment, consistency, caring, self-reflection, and self-control.

Children who live these values *expect* to succeed, no matter what the task. As a result, they handle pressure well, and they persist in working toward their goals. But we have to believe in them first. Remember the little train that labored up the hill and finally announced, "I thought I could, I thought I could"? Well, you can feel certain that sitting on a side track somewhere, Momma Train was agreeing with him, "I thought you could, too."

2. *Use Role Models.* Children have to copy the behaviors of successful people, especially of their parents. If they do, they soon discover, as you and I have, that people who act like winners, especially if they do it often enough, eventually *become* winners. They develop good habits: a sense of purpose, perseverance, teamwork, responsibility, a healthy aggressiveness. Losers don't do these things. That's why, according to the old coaching maxim, "Losers lose, and winners win."

3. *Learn to Listen.* Successful people listen actively and aggressively. They want to hear what others have to say because they know that they might learn something. Listeners are learners, and learners are winners. They also learn from unsuccessful attempts. They transform losing into resiliency by correcting mistakes and by realizing that every adversity overcome makes success more possible. One of our roles as parents, therefore, is to be good listeners and make good listeners of our kids.

4. *Have a sense of purpose.* Another role is to help our kids reflect on and judge their own behavior, identify their weaknesses, and determine how to correct them. We have to help them establish goals and persist in working toward them, and we can't give them excuses for failure. We have to be sensitive to their developmental needs, but we must not enable them by being overly sensitive.

How about the high school out west that prohibited kids from playing tag? They justified their decision by asserting that kids who were "it" would feel victimized and lose self-esteem.

Our job is to help our children establish challenging goals and to hold their feet to the fire when trying to accomplish them. If we help them learn from their failures, they can dare greatly because they won't *be* failures unless they quit trying. Challenging goals, persistence, and confidence in the resilience of our children—these are powerful keys to success.

5. *Don't let success get in your way.* Success is like driving a car. If you don't stay focused on the task at hand, you'll end up in a ditch somewhere. Successful

drivers sustain a focus on their performance—the act of driving the car carefully. They don't allow thoughts of their destinations to distract them. Similarly, successful athletes don't allow winning to interfere with the performance of their skills. Success gets in the way of future performances when accomplishment is taken for granted. Smart parents and good coaches understand, therefore, that one of their primary roles is to encourage the child's effort over the outcome of the contest.

Parents must never allow winning to be the exclusive goal of any kind of competition. Commitment, continued effort, constant improvement, these are the immediate goals of children, no matter what they do. On the field or court, the outcome of the contest will take care of itself if kids do a good job executing their responsibilities and skills. In the classroom, the grade will take care of itself if they study hard.

Finally, once the goal is accomplished, another important role of parents is to be sure that kids always ask themselves: "Exactly what was it that got me here?" Self-reflection is a critical skill for young people. Once they reflect often enough on successful experiences, you can be sure that they won't say it was luck "that got them there." More likely, they'll say "hard work," "cooperating with my teammates and coaches," "thinking positive thoughts," and "refusing to quit." Such an answer re-enforces their good habits and results in a recommitment to the behaviors that lead to success.

Help Children Make Their Own Decisions

Choosing the sport is just one decision kids have to make. They also have to decide to give it their best shot and to make sure that it doesn't interfere with their other responsibilities. Youngsters involved in sports are called "student athletes." "Student" is the operative word. Every decision they make about sports must recognize their primary responsibility as students and family members.

Said one coach, "Emphasis on academics has deteriorated along with respect, integrity, and other values. Some [athletes] only aim low, to go to a junior college. They don't aim high. Too many kids want to be great in basketball but mediocre in other things. They make excuses rather than strive to excel."

Consider the fact that in a recent year only three public league athletes in Chicago met the NCAA's requirements to play Division I basketball. Too many kids, especially in the inner cities, see basketball as the road to immediate financial and personal success. They don't realize that only a fraction of high school basketball players ever play in the pros.

The problem isn't restricted to the inner cities. Sports, especially for gifted youngsters, can consume all of a child's time. The experiences can be so satisfying that they obscure academic and family responsibilities. When helping children decide on a sport, therefore, our role is to make sure they also reflect on the place of that sport in their lives. Cover these nine questions with them. Specifically, ask them: As an athlete, are you willing to:

- work hard and commit to your teammates and coaches?

- stay healthy and fit by following the training rules?

- work hard in practice?

- attend every practice?

- put academics before athletics?

- find time to be a family member and do all that is expected of you at home?

- use language that shows good breeding?

- cooperate with, support, and respect your teammates and share responsibilities.

Being a Good Spectator

Kids have their responsibilities as athletes, and we have responsibilities when watching them. Being a good spectator is one of your most important roles. Sports psychologists tell us repeatedly that parent misbehavior is one of the biggest problems at contests.

To guarantee a wholesome experience for your children at all contests, parents are well-advised to:

- Remember that admission to a sporting contest is a privilege.

- Stay in your seats throughout the contest.

- Avoid making instructional or critical comments to your child, other children, opposing parents, or contest officials.

- Applaud outstanding performances, no matter who on the field or court makes them.

- Recognize your child's coach as the only person who determines strategy and player selection.

The parent's role has other responsibilities as well. When I was coaching, I discussed the following with parents at early informational meetings. I asked parents to:

- accompany their children to as many orientation and informational meetings as possible,

- work closely with all program and school personnel to guarantee academic as well as athletic experiences for their children,

- promise that their children will attend all scheduled practices and contests,

- help their children follow the training rules,

- work closely with coaches and school personnel to plan realistic futures for student athletes,

- avoid the use of tobacco and alcohol during contests,

- recognize that violations of important guidelines will subject spectators to ejection from contests.

These are reasonable expectations of parents. It's no startling revelation to say that sports are for kids, that our job as parents is to assure that kids benefit from the experience. That won't happen when parents, unfortunately most of them are dads, steal the sports spotlight by making spectacles of themselves in the stands. Some of them really have no idea just how embarrassing they are to their children, families, and fellow spectators.

Don't Be Asked to Leave. Schools across the country are ejecting unruly and childish parents from contests. Some of us feel it's about time. Parents inclined to abusive and immature behavior are well-advised to keep this in mind. They're also reminded that many schools and youth programs punish repeat offenders by barring them from all contests for the remainder of the season or school year.

From the Opinion page of a suburban newspaper: "I'm thankful that my years with this [baseball youth] program are coming to an end. I would never recommend this program to any new residents. I think there are too many people involved who have forgotten the purpose of the league, and have as their only priority to win at any expense. Too many fathers are living their own unachieved dreams through this organization. Unfortunately, it is at the expense of their own children; it will no longer be at the expense of mine."

Pretty strong words. This is a sad and revealing commentary on the state of many youth programs in this country. It also is a condemnation of the behavior of many parents. Written by a mother, it points out the need for essential change in many of these programs as well as in the behaviors of parents.

Listen to your mother. Admittedly, it's a mother's perspective, and, let's admit it, mothers look at sports differently from fathers. I learned a long time ago to listen carefully to this perspective. Other good coaches have learned to do the same thing. Consider legendary basketball coach Ray Meyer. When seeking players at DePaul University in Chicago, he once said, "When you recruit a player, you recruit the mom."

Wrote columnist and DePaul "Insider" Toni Ginnetti, ". . . whether he knew it or not, Meyer was a 'mom coach.' Which distinguishes him from those who are a 'dad coach.' 'Mom coaches'—[they're] a little more patient, a little less volatile, a lot more civil."

Remember who has the power. Meyer understood that the role of parents, in this instance mothers, is also to keep an eye on coaches to make sure they are "doing right" by their sons and daughters. If coaches are the least bit abusive, that role also requires them to criticize or seek to change the coach's behavior, either that or tell her child not to play for that coach. Meyer understood that, in that regard, the role of parent can have far more power than most people realize.

Said George Kelly, long-time assistant coach at the University of Nebraska, and later at Notre Dame: "The media and many parents think we, as college coaches, have all the power when it comes to offering scholarships and recruiting players. What many of them forget is that if they say no to us, our program is in trouble. That's power!"

Okay, dads, let's be honest. Sometimes we want certain coaches to work with our kids "to toughen them up" or "to pound a little discipline into them." Having coached for thirty-one years and having seen more than my share of undisciplined brats slip on the pads, I understand the occasional need to be a hard-liner. So do some moms. Toni Ginnetti agrees. She wrote further, "Of course, there are moms who might prefer 'dad coaches,' because they are concerned their sons might need a stronger hand. And there are dads who might just as well go for the 'mom' approach."

Look for "mom coaches" in youth programs. Obviously, it's a matter of style. Good "mom coaches" win just as often as good "dad coaches." What is especially true, however, is that the "mom coach's" philosophy—patient, controlled, and civil—is needed for youth programs. The younger the athlete, the more humane the treatment must be. Professional, college, even some high school athletes can respond to tough, in-your-face coaching styles, but children require gentler treatment. Our role as parents is make sure they get it.

I wrote in an earlier book, "The red-faced, bellowing drill sergeant who thunders up and down the sidelines bringing 300-pound giants to their emotional knees may be a winner in much of our folklore, but in the real world he loses more often than he wins."

Older kids, even women and men, require understanding. Without it, they are unable to make a consistent, maximum effort. Athletes, no matter how good, can't contend with opposing players *and* their own coach. As important, we all know that it's hard to learn from someone who yells all the time. We tune them out. Good parents understand this, so do good coaches. The smart coach uses a raised voice judiciously. He or she realizes that it works only occasionally, for effect.

No child wants to establish a relationship with someone who yells all the time. This book has indicated several times that an athlete's peak performance depends on positive thinking and a clear focus on performance. Both unlikely in an atmosphere strained by loud criticism. This is especially true of young children, and many simply are not finding the relationships they need. The study at Michigan State University offers several explanations. One is especially noteworthy.

Michigan State's research was originally entitled "Participation and Attrition Patterns in American Agency-Sponsored and Interscholastic Sports." Fortunately, the media decided to call it the "Dropout Study." All the research done by MSU's Youth Sports Institute was funded by the Athletic Footwear Association (AFA). The study had a big impact on the thinking of coaches and parents and suggests several important points for all of us.

One point stands out. Gary Brown, the executive director of AFA, observed, "Perhaps our coaches are good at teaching physical skills, but not terribly well-versed in the psychology of sports. It suggests we need to focus more attention on coaching the person, as well as the athlete." Good coaches have known this for a long time, but it bears repeating. Kids need character as well as skills to be winners, and good coaches help them develop both.

Dealing with inferior coaches. Some coaches don't seek to build character. Some aren't even very good at teaching basic skills, let alone advanced skills. Our role as parents is to make sure that coaches look beyond simplistic definitions of their jobs and begin to understand and meet their responsibilities. We can't do that simply by criticizing them at home or shouting at them in the stands. In fact, when we do that, we abuse them as much as many of them abuse our kids.

What we can do is join with other concerned parents to develop standards to guide coaching behaviors, then display the standards prominently in

Little League or Pop Warner offices. If our kids are in high school, we meet with personnel from the athletic department to identify the school's standards and to suggest ways to get coaches to use them as guides for establishing relationships with young athletes.

The supervision and evaluation of coaches work if done well, but neither is done routinely with coaches, especially in youth programs. We can help if we assume the role of recognizing and commending coaches who do relate to our children as persons, not just as athletes. And this doesn't involve the development of a Hall of Fame, maybe just a Wall of Fame in an office somewhere.

Your role as a parent, therefore, may involve nothing more than handing out certificates and putting plaques on walls, anything that identifies and recognizes coaches who work consistently to satisfy the standards established by parents and league or school authorities. Post the standards and the names of award recipients prominently in offices, community centers, locker rooms, and elsewhere so that coaches are constantly reminded of the behaviors expected of them. This is a simple yet very effective way to encourage coaches to handle the complicated task of helping kids grow and to go above and beyond any thoughts of *merely* winning. Some sample standards:

- Years of service, usually more than ten.

- Win-loss record. It may not involve more wins than losses, just a respectable total. One hundred wins is often the standard.

- Models adult behavior.

- Creates a positive learning experience.

- Recognizes and demonstrates that effort is more important than outcome.

- Helps kids focus and learn to control anger and stress.

- Helps young athletes develop positive self-concepts.

- Recognizes the needs of young athletes on and off the field or court.

- Works willingly with parents and league or school authorities.

- Works harder on developing the character of athletes than on winning.

It's important that coaches and parents talk to each other. Even more important is that they listen to each other. Open lines of communication between coaches and parents are essential if kids are to learn from their athletic experiences. When I coached, our program rivaled the Pentagon for its informational meetings and briefings.

When I first started to coach, a friend of mine, a veteran for twenty-five years, told me, "A word of advice; listen more than you talk. I've watched too many good coaches die by elocution. It's a tough way to go."

We knew that parents needed to share their concerns. I learned early in my coaching career that the athletic ability of their child was their greatest concern. Most wanted their child to have more playing time. Some parents were also concerned about strategy, so we as coaches always found time to discuss these concerns, either in a group or individually with parents. To be honest, we rarely compromised with parents because we felt that we were more objective about the abilities of their kids and knew more about game or contest strategy.

A quick guideline: The younger the child, the more playing time he or she should have. At the beginning level, all children should have equal playing time. As kids get older, they and their parents should recognize that contributions at practice are as important as contributions during contests.

But we also knew that we had to talk about these issues. We knew that if we didn't, the concerns would spill out in the stands or at cocktail parties on weekends and nothing would be accomplished but some generalized venting. We knew, however, that there was a right way and a wrong way to discuss these issues, so we asked parents to:

- Try not to make overtly critical comments in the stands or elsewhere in the community. Share them with us personally.

- Not approach us with concerns in front of the kids. It's best to discuss areas of concern when the kids are not around.

- Make sure we treat each other with mutual respect, especially when we disagree.

- Work cooperatively to solve problems. Whenever we disagree, we have identified a problem.

- Above all, remember that we are not adversaries. The closer we cooperate with each other, the more the kids will gain from the program.

Keep these five suggestions in mind when talking about sports with your kids:

1. Listen more than you talk. We have to know what our child's opinions and feelings are before we can do anything about them.

2. In that regard, good questions are more important than good answers. They open the door to meaningful communication and help kids focus on issues that are or *should be* important to them.

3. Your feelings about athletics are less important than your child's. What you did or hoped to do as an athlete are less important than what your child wants.

4. Your child's mistakes are rarely times for criticism. They are *always* times for learning.

5. Always help your child focus on the fact that winning is much less important than *making the effort* to win.

Let's Wrap It Up

The role of the parent in sports is important but often frustrating. Probably most frustrating is our constant struggle to avoid getting over-involved with our kids or their coaches. Two of my daughters were deeply involved in sports and, although they thank me now for my earlier involvement, I know that I stepped over the line more than once. I know that they know it, too. I wanted them to be so successful that I know that I put undue pressure on them and sometimes forgot my college coach's advice: "Never pass up the opportunity to keep your mouth shut."

But, in fairness to myself and to all those parents out there, I know how hard it is to keep your mouth shut when kids or coaches seem desperately in need of advice. But I've learned that it is precisely at those times when I most need to say something that I should say nothing. Keeping quiet is much easier if we keep in mind that kids join sports to have fun, learn skills, and make friends. The desire to win is much less important to them.

And it should be. Winning is a goal in sports, but not the most important goal. I can't count the number of times I have said to kids at halftime: "Boys, winning or losing this game is unimportant. All that matters when you take the field for the second half is that you commit yourself to each other, remember your assignments, and make a maximum effort. After the game, know that you gave it your best shot."

That's all they can do. Their role is clear cut. So is ours—because that's all we can expect of them.

3.
CONDITIONING AND THE YOUNG ATHLETE

Did You Know?

- Michael Jordan was originally cut from his high school basketball team.

- My grandfather Jim Thorpe was only 5'4" and 115 pounds when he entered the Carlisle Indian School at the age of fourteen.

- Wilma Rudolph, one of history's greatest Olympic track athletes, was bedridden for two years as a child.

- The winner of the most Olympic gold medals (ten), Ray Ewry, was an invalid as a child.

Perseverance and a good conditioning program can work miracles. The human body is an amazing machine that routinely rewards hard work and commitment, no matter what its initial condition. My thirty years of coaching were populated by scores of little, overweight wannabes who were so consumed by the spectacle and tradition of football that they actually thought they could play the game—and they did. Some even went on to play in college.

All of them enjoyed what biologists call a symbiotic relationship with sports. They committed to sports, and sports committed to them. Our football program was better because of them, and they were better because of our football program. Sports does much more than simply improve the physical conditioning of young athletes. It also improves self-esteem and energizes the child's emotional balance and attention level so that learning is improved.

Youngsters who condition themselves because of their involvement in sports programs, therefore, gain much more than a strong body and a few plaques on their walls. Sports engage youngsters emotionally as well as cognitively and physically. It is this emotional involvement that increases attention levels, just one reason why so many parents marvel at the fact that junior completely understands an "inside-belly-counter-tackle trap at five versus the gap stack forty-four" when, earlier, he struggled with gerunds and participles.

The good news is that emotionally charged attention levels can find their way off the field or court and into the classroom. Kids carry elevated attention levels with them wherever they go. The increased awareness provoked by sports is also evident in the fine arts, indeed in any activities where movement, physical or mental, is required. They expand children's awareness and open them up to experiences of all kinds, including gerunds and participles.

Wasn't it Yogi Berra who said, "Baseball is 90 percent mental. The other half is physical"?

Equally important is the fact that physical activity also increases levels of endorphin and serotonin, neurotransmitters that enhance self-esteem and actually reduce the irritability that often causes aggressive, reckless, violent, and sometimes suicidal behavior. Universities and research labs across the country are studying the relationship of exercise to serotonin output. Unfortunately, the verdict is still out because the brain's output is difficult to measure. Most researchers continue the study, however, because they are convinced that exercise enhances the output of both endorphins and serotonin.

And there is no doubt within the medical community that serotonin enhances self-esteem and social ease, that it inhibits impulsive behaviors and leads to the calm self-assurance that is so important, not only to good athletes but to well-balanced people. Sports programs, then, promote levels of physical activity that have far reaching benefits, only a small part of which involve scoring touchdowns or hitting home runs.

But any program of physical conditioning must be undertaken carefully, especially by young athletes. The road to excellent physical condition and athletic excellence involves potentially dangerous twists and turns. Injury awaits young athletes around every corner. Parents must help them travel the road carefully, fully aware of the right way and the wrong way to reach their destinations.

The Growth and Development of Young Athletes

For the moment, forget about having fun, making new friends, and learning skills. These are the benefits kids want from sports, and they'll find them if you and the coaches do your jobs. But sports provide a whole lot more for your children, including the impulse control and improved learning kids gain from exercise and the chemical reactions it creates within their bodies. But a word to the wise, don't encourage them to go out for a sport because it will "actualize their cognitive potential." Let's keep that our little secret.

A Few Facts About Growth: First and most important, children's bones, because they are still growing, are not as strong as yours. The growth plates found at the end of the bones are usually weaker than the tendons and ligaments that connect the bones. In addition, the growth spurts of most kids, which can last up to two to three years, cause problems with muscles and tendons. They don't grow as fast as bones, which results in decreased flexibility for most kids and a stronger likelihood of serious injury.

Years ago, these facts were relatively unimportant. Sports didn't make the same kinds of demands on kids' bodies they do today. Youngsters are now playing one or more organized sports year-round. Some are trying to meet the unique demands of elite competition well before their growth is complete. Gymnastics, ice skating, tennis, even hockey are consuming kids' lives and doing all kinds of potential damage to their bodies.

Said one orthopedist in a recent newspaper article: "Kids' bodies just aren't made for it. [I saw a young baseball pitcher] with the elbow of an 80-year-old, and I've seen injuries to young long-distance runners in which the rim of the pelvis pulls off at a growth plate."

Orthopedists indicate that growing numbers of physical problems among kids are the result of overuse, not injury or accident. The intensity of competition and the accompanying demands on kids' bodies have increased so dramatically within the past few years that orthopedists are sharing their concerns with the media. Fortunately, many of them are reporting that overuse problems are not difficult to diagnose. They involve obvious and recurring warning signals.

Make sure kids heed them. The key is to make sure kids pay attention to these warning signals. Most kids have learned from college and professional athletes and, let's admit it, from a few inexperienced but zealous coaches, that "playing with pain" is a sign of toughness. What youngster putting on the pads for the first time doesn't want to be tough? They've also discovered that giving in to aches and pains can lose starting positions and chances to play in big games. Dedicated and committed kids don't like that, so they learn to tolerate the subtle but lingering pains that might signal serious physical problems.

A friend, himself a former college athlete, tells the story of his daughter, a very promising junior high basketball player. Cindy's career ended before high school. She ignored what later was diagnosed as a stress fracture in one of her growth plates. Her leg grew crooked, and she still walks with a slight limp.

The responsibility of parents, then, is to understand and demand one unequivocal rule when it comes to all aspects of physical conditioning and competition for kids. *If it hurts, stop!* "Play through pain," and "No pain, no gain," are dumb advice for young athletes. Most kids are so wrapped up in the excitement and tradition of the games they love that they'll do anything to keep playing them.

They've also been conditioned by years of folklore. Great athletes are tough. They tolerate pain. They even play with broken limbs. What most kids fail to realize is that when such athletes leave the spotlight most of them can't even put on their own socks or get up from the dining room table. They live with pain and spend more time with the family doctor than with their wives and kids.

Most of these athletes *needed* to win. They placed such a high priority on winning that they surrendered their bodies to their athletic goals. This is yet another example of how *needing* to win is as bad as *wanting* to win is good. We want our children to focus on performance in an attempt to win. We don't want them to risk lifelong injury or compromise anything else in their lives to satisfy the *need* to win. "Win at all costs" is not an option for our kids.

Just say no. Prominent people are reminding kids every day to "just say no" to drugs. It's good advice for parents, too, but in a different way. Closely monitor your child's participation in sports, and if you observe signs of pain, don't hesitate to find the origin. If necessary, take your child to the family doctor for a diagnosis. If the pain signals potential problems and the child wants to play in spite of them—just say no! It's that simple. Saying no to playing with pain will anger your child now, but—if you can wait long enough—it will involve a "thank you" years from now.

Development is more than just growth. Kids can influence growth with proper nutrition and a humane exercise program, but much of what they will be in later adolescence and adulthood is genetically predetermined. In fact, current research indicates that at least 2,000 diseases and disorders are linked to our individual genetic codes. That most kids resemble their parents is evident in every sport's preseason informational meeting. But the medical community assures us that genetics is not the only influence on appearance.

For example, although obesity tends to run in families, a commitment to regular exercise and a sensible diet can prevent it. How well kids want to perform athletically, therefore, is up to them. The better their nutritional and conditioning habits, the more likely they will break a certain chain of genetic predispositions and accomplish many of their sports goals.

A little honesty goes a long way. We as parents, however, have to help kids keep things in perspective. Certainly, we don't want to step all over our child's dreams, but we also know that it's important to keep all of our goals in perspective. Rigorous conditioning will overcome our physical limitations just so much. Most of us have enjoyed Charles Schulz's "Peanuts" comic strip for years, and we've come to enjoy Charlie Brown's unabashed love of baseball. But even the most optimistic among us know that he will never be a big-league pitcher.

I have never recommended telling a child that he or she couldn't do something. Kids have surprised me too many times. Some have gone so far beyond my predictions for them that I was embarrassed by my own foolish assessments of their ability. But I also want them to be happy and to avoid the frustration and disappointment that accompany an unrealistic goal. So my advice to kids has always been: "Go for it! Shoot for the moon—but be happy if you only hit the top of the barn."

Once again, the emphasis is on performance over outcome. Kids must realize that the effort they put into a task is more important than the outcome. That little cherub who enchants the entire family with the sparkle of her smile and personality should commit to a conditioning program to improve her appearance, fitness, and athletic skills, not to chase a dream that she will be an Olympic high jumper. Her emphasis on performance and conditioning may result in self-discipline, a commitment to hard work, and health and fitness improvements. An exclusive emphasis on being an Olympic high jumper, however, may result only in frustration and disappointment.

Three Steps to Developing Athletic Skills

The child's growth and development are the most important factors in any competitive physical activity. Needless injury is becoming too commonplace among young athletes. Also important, however, is the child's skill development as an athlete. Children who develop solid fundamental skills not only compete successfully, but also avoid unnecessary injury. It's essential that parents understand how kids develop these skills in order to provide help at important times. The development of any athletic skills involves three steps:

Thinking. Every skill, no matter what sport, involves techniques that enable athletes to compete successfully and safely. The more parents know about these skills, the more they can help their children, especially their young children, think about and develop them. Most parents play catch, shoot baskets, or kick balls with their children long before the kids join organized sports programs. Few parents are able to teach advanced skills, but most can provide introductory experiences that are fun and basically instructive.

The first step requires that the child understands the purpose and execution of the skill. Although this step is brief, it is important because it provides demonstrations, explanations, and feedback from parents and coaches. A child's first few attempts to catch a ball usually receive only cheers and high fives. Continuing attempts may receive positive but instructive feedback. Parents must understand that these first attempts are important because they provide the foundation for the child's future growth as an athlete.

"Walk before you run!"

Every athletic skill involves principles that are so basic that parents, even coaches, sometimes take them for granted. But they are essential if children are to improve and develop advanced skills. "Look the ball into your hands." "Keep your eye on the ball." These are simple but fundamental skills young children must develop to learn and to enjoy any game with a ball.

Older, more experienced kids must learn to "Stay squared up to the basket." "Make a swan; feel the ball roll off your finger tips." "Follow through on your pass." "Don't *aim* the pitch; *feel* it." These, too, are basic skills, but they are appropriate for kids who have been playing the sport for a while and are able to understand the purpose of the instruction. The key is to understand, learn, and master these fundamentals in order to play the sport successfully and safely and to learn advanced skills.

Thinking and Doing. The second step involves thinking about the skills, but, more importantly, *doing* them—over and over again. Most practice sessions involve *drills*, sessions that involve young athletes in the constant repetition of the skill so that it becomes fixed in their mind's and their body's memory. Parents are important at this stage because they can provide the support kids need to understand and enjoy such repetitive activity. Playing catch or shooting baskets on the driveway is one way to provide such support for young kids.

"Perfect practice makes perfect."

For older children who are involved in organized sports programs, parents who show interest and recognize dedication and hard work provide important support. Obviously, especially for older kids, this second step lasts much longer than the first, and it can be more tedious.

One summer I decided to pump weights with the team. My exercise routine had dwindled to nothing more than lifting my legs when my wife vacuumed. While pushing the team clown one day, I emphasized the importance of working on bench presses. He agreed with me but had to add, "Yeah, but can't I do this by correspondence course?!"

Drilling skills into the body's memory takes time and constant feedback. Without both time and feedback, however, young athletes fail to master important skills and are unprepared for step three. More importantly, they jeopardize their ability to learn advanced skills and to play the game successfully—and *safely*. And a correspondence course won't get that done.

Unthinking. Only after the first two steps have been accomplished is the young athlete ready to accomplish step three. This step involves the performance of the skill without thinking about it. The skill has been practiced so often that the young athlete performs it spontaneously. As a matter of fact, at this point the skill is so routine that conscious thought usually interferes with its execution.

"Trust your body!"

To quote Yogi Berra again, "You can't think and hit at the same time." Needless to say, everyone within earshot laughed, convinced they had heard another of Yogi's memorable malaprops. What most of them gained in entertainment value, however, they lost in good, solid advice. A good hitter can't hit and think at the same time, nor can a basketball player think the ball through the hoop. Divers can't think about double somersaults; gymnasts can't think about back walkovers. They have to feel them; they have to trust their bodies to execute such skills spontaneously. In fact, the more they *do* think about such skills, especially at critical times, the more they "choke" and fail to execute them.

So, although these are pointers used by most good coaches, parents must understand them, too. They are simple but important pieces of advice that parents can reinforce at home, not just because they enhance the child's performance, but because they are so important to the child's safety and self-image.

Nutrition for Young Athletes: Using the Right Fuel

Telling parents about kids and food is like telling a mechanic about cars and gas. I won't be so presumptuous, but I do like the analogy. Muscles are the body's engine. Without the right fuel, they "run out of gas" and lose essential energy. Although any kind of gas will keep the engine running, only the best mix can guarantee peak performance. Proper nutrition is critical to young athletes, maybe more important than any other formative influence on them because of its impact on lifelong health habits. It also is the influence over which parents have the most control. Certainly, no one expects you to understand that fat is a series of carbon molecules with hydrogen and oxygen molecules attached along the chain. More important is the knowledge that fats provide energy in combination with the sugars that release it. Most important is the fact that a proper diet improves athletic performance and has lasting value for kids through life.

Nutrition and Common Sense: Most kids can develop an appetite just by opening the refrigerator door. That they are almost constantly hungry is no stunning revelation to most parents, but it's especially true after vigorous exercise. The key for parents is to make sure their children replace energy lost through exercise with energy gained through sound nutrition. Fast food after practice isn't the answer. It represents the lowest octane gas kids can put in their tanks.

Yes, yes, I know, compared to you and me, kids can handle the occasional cheeseburger. Exercise elevates their metabolism to the point where they convert it quickly into energy. The same French fry that latches on immediately to our hips, thighs, and stomach finds its way to the muscles of an active child. That's the good news. But the bad news about fast food is that, if used too often, it fails to provide the building blocks young athletes need to repair and promote the growth of damaged and overworked muscles.

Vigorous exercise and the continuing demands of a growing body can take a lot out of kids, but a well-balanced diet can put it all back. In fact, a well-balanced diet has been recommended for a long time.

> *"The harder you work an engine, the more fuel it requires. When a man is trying to build himself up by means of exercise, he simply has to take enough food to repair the tissue which is broken down while exercising. . . . Most of the men who are noted for their strength eat three meals a day, and their diet is a mixed one. I believe that a mixed diet is the best one for an athlete."*

"Mixed diet"—"well-balanced diet"—not much has changed over the years. This quote was taken from an article titled, "Body-Building and Muscle-Developing Exercise." It was published by the Milo Barbell Company almost *90 years ago*. That parents provide a well-balanced diet for their kids, therefore, is sanctioned by time and good, common sense.

The Three Building Blocks of a Strong Body: The building blocks of a strong body are the same building blocks adults use to maintain good fitness and health:

1. *Fat.* The media have convinced us that fat causes everything from clogged arteries to lousy self-images, and they're right. But fat is also essential for meeting our energy needs. It's important for all of

us and can be found abundantly, if not exclusively, in meat and dairy products. Without some fat in the diet, young athletes can't meet the demands of practice or competition.

Folks who starve daily to eliminate body fat may not realize that the brain is fatty. Fat can also be our friend!

---

2. *Carbohydrates.* Found in food starches and sugars, carbohydrates provide immediate energy. Potatoes are rich in starch and other nutrients. Sucrose found in table sugar, fructose found in fruits, and lactose found in milk are rich sources of sugars and are essential nutrients for athletes because of their important energy supplies. Athletes who run out of sugars during practice or competition hit the proverbial "wall." They not only fail to perform, but subject themselves to injury and other serious problems.

I mentioned this fact to a friend recently. He told me, "Yes, I know. I learned the hard way. The first machine my health club put me on was the respirator."

That enjoyable but much maligned chocolate bar is quick energy for kids, but slow death for the rest of us. Without regular exercise, candy is stored in the body as fat. So while bon-bons and chocolate doughnuts sit in our fat cells waiting for us to "get moving," they replenish important energy supplies for active kids. This is not to say that a floor littered with candy wrappers is a sign of physical fitness, not even for kids. A balanced diet of carbohydrates and other nutrients is still the answer.

> *After vigorous exercise, the heart absorbs all these quick energy supplies before any other muscle in the body. Mother Nature helps the heart replenish its supply first in the event strenuous exercise is needed again. Once the heart gets its share, it lets the others have theirs.*

3. *Proteins.* Proteins are needed to help muscles grow and to repair them after vigorous exercise. It's also important to note that most antibodies, our partners in fighting infection, are proteins. The meat (including fish), eggs, and beans that most kids enjoy so much, therefore, provide the proteins that not only help build them up, but prevent illness from breaking them down.

> *Most young athletes continue to burn calories after vigorous exercise. The process of repairing the small muscle tears that result from strain requires energy.*

Vitamins, minerals, and water are also necessary building blocks because they transport food products to tissues and carry waste products from them. They are important for other reasons as well, but even the most active young athletes will get all the minerals and vitamins they need if they eat a well-balanced diet. Such a diet provides proteins to develop and repair muscles and carbohydrates to provide for energy. An emphasis on one over the other fails to meet all the needs of young athletes.

For example, the recent emphasis on "carbo loading" that filled so many athletes' plates with fruits, vegetables, and pastas may have helped meet their energy needs, but it fell short of developing and repairing the muscles they needed to compete successfully. On the other hand, those few body builders who focused exclusively on protein diets developed muscle, but ran out of gas during vigorous exercise.

Six Myths About Nutrition

Here's some good news and some bad news about nutrition. These myths apply to you as well as that young athlete in the house. Most of these are borrowed from my earlier book, *Building the Total Athlete*, written with my son-in-law, Bruce Hanson. First the good news:

1. *Only vigorous exercise burns calories.* False! You'll be pleased to know that any increase in activity burns calories. None of us likes to vacuum, but the good news is that it can burn up to 150 calories. A round of golf will burn up to 600; even four hours of typing will burn 100.

2. *Seafood helps reduce cholesterol in the diet.* Right! *But* (there's always a "but"), whereas some fish, especially those with white meat are low in fat and cholesterol, others are high in fat. And if you like an appetizer of fried calamari while dining with friends and family, you'll take in more cholesterol than you'll find on a plate full of bacon and eggs.

3. *Pasta is a good health food.* True! Spaghetti and other pastas are great sources of carbohydrates, but the sauces layered on them can have as much saturated fat as three pints of chocolate ice cream. So if you or your child wants to lose weight, eat the pasta but stay away from the Alfredo sauce.

Now the bad news:

4. *Dieting makes our stomachs shrink.* False. You may not get as bloated as from over-eating, but your stomach always stays approximately the same size. But you'll shrink. That's the good news.

5. *Fasting loses weight permanently.* Not so. Most of the weight lost during fasting is water and muscle tissue. The only effective way to lose weight? A lifetime of moderate exercise and a well-balanced, well-maintained diet.

When you fast, your body actually tries to store more fat to protect itself from future diets!

---

6. *Lots of salt prevents cramps.* No! Any cramping that occurs during vigorous exercise results from water loss. The idea of taking salt to prevent cramping is one of the sports world's biggest myths. Once kids take salt, their bodies rush water to the salt instead of to their muscles, where they need it most. There's only one way to stop cramping—drink water, lots of it.

Young athletes and parents must understand that extreme weight loss is a serious problem for many athletes, especially boxers, wrestlers, gymnasts, and others. The need to "make weight" often results in a level of fasting that actually makes the body feed on itself by breaking down its own proteins. What most kids fail to understand is that this results in a loss of muscle tissue and strength. Kids who want to lose weight quickly are well-advised to see the family doctor for an effective and safe program and to lose it gradually.

The same is true of athletes who want to gain weight. Athletes in all sports, especially in football and basketball, are getting bigger every day. Whereas a 300-pounder in football was once rare, it's now commonplace. Many college teams boast an offensive line that averages well over 300 pounds. One result is that young athletes feel the need to bulk up in order to play these games. Some kids believe this so strongly that their idea of heavy lifting is carrying their lunch to school each day.

Certainly, it's an advantage for linemen to be big, just as it's good for basketball players to be tall, but a child's health is more important than the requirements of a sport. Youngsters, and this includes secondary and college-level athletes, who "fatten up" to "fit in" risk serious health problems. Immoderate eating can cause problems with the kidneys, the heart, and other organs, especially if combined with steroid or other drug use. Exercise and a well-balanced diet are still the only answers to good health and successful athletic performance.

Sherry Baron, conducting a study for the National Institute of Occupational Safety and Health, discovered recently that large NFL linemen are 52 percent more likely to die of heart disease than the general public. She also found that players who aren't linemen are 52 percent less likely.

Weight Training: Good and Bad

Back in the Stone Age—when I played football—a barbell was a block of cement and a dumbbell was anyone who tried to lift it. Weight training was an occasional push away from the dinner table. It may have done wonders for my waistline, but it didn't do much for my shoulder and neck strength. My football career ended with a cerebral hemorrhage at Nebraska. As I look back on it, it was a direct result of poor weight training.

I learned the hard way that a good weight training program not only improves performance, but prevents serious injury. Thirty-one years of coaching reinforced that reality for me. The weight program that we required of our kids during the summer months worked miracles for hundreds of them over the years. Joint injuries, so prevalent during my first few years of coaching, were virtually eliminated for the remainder of my coaching career. We may have had the occasional knee or ankle injury, but far fewer from anything I had experienced as a player or young coach.

During my fourth year of coaching, we were concerned that five players had shoulder separations during the past season. The injuries signaled the start of our weight training program. For my next twenty-seven years of coaching, we didn't have one shoulder separation.

When Weight Lifting Helps, and When It Doesn't. Obviously, weight lifting is most helpful for strengthening joints to prevent injury and to enhance performance. The stronger the athlete, the less likely she or he is to experience traumatic injury—if the program accommodates the strength needs of the athlete, is tailored to meet the specific demands of the sport, and requires the athlete to work on all vital areas of the body. Looking good on the beach is more important for some kids than strengthening their bodies for athletic competition.

Several years ago, we had our first really big lineman. He was 6'7" and weighed 310 pounds—as a high school junior! Needless to say, scores of colleges were knocking on his door. We tried hard to get him to work on his legs because of the weight he was carrying, but every time we turned our backs, he did curls to make his arms bigger. Early in his senior year, he severely twisted his right knee, missed two weeks of practice, eventually returned, and promptly tore cartilage in his other knee. He missed the entire season and never got to play in college.

Weight training is helpful, then, but only if done properly. A poorly organized weight program can itself cause injuries. Parents are well-advised to check with a coach or another professional before allowing your child, especially your young child, to lift weights. Consider just a few reasons:

- The bodies of most youngsters haven't fully developed. Their growth plates are still maturing. Severe strain on these areas of the body can cause lifelong debility. *This point is critically important.* Far too many kids start lifting weights too early in life. The damage they do their bodies sometimes ends their playing careers prematurely and often causes nagging pain well into adulthood.

- Most kids, even a few older ones, are too competitive when lifting weights. Everyone tries to lift as much as the strongest person on the team. Weight lifting must be viewed by kids as a purely individual activity. Kids must be taught to compete only against themselves, setting personal goals and trying to improve on them.

- Most children fail to use proper form. Because they try to lift too much weight, they don't lift properly, and they fail to benefit from the program. Some will even quit because of the frustration and pain they cause themselves.

- Children lifting alone don't have spotters to help them. Someone must always be on hand to help a child if the weight slips or if the child gets injured. Spotters are also important for a little cheerleading support!

- Most kids aren't completely sure *why* they're lifting weights. Many simply want to "look good" and fail to do the exercises that prevent injury.

There are a lot more potential problems when kids start to lift for the first time. Again, be sure to get the best advice from professionals. Parents who race out to buy a weight set because their child wants to start lifting may be leading her into serious injury.

Flexibility: Injury prevention is more important to us as parents than our child's improved performance. We all want our kids to be the best they can be, so we do everything in our power to help them. One of the best pieces of advice we can give is to have them work as hard on flexibility as they do on anything else. Weight lifting tends to tighten muscles, to shorten them. That's why it's important for young athletes to stretch them to assure maximum flexibility.

Inflexible muscles tear and rip, causing pain and extensive recovery time. Think of the muscle as a rubber band that stretches without breaking. The more flexible the stretch, the more snap it has and the better its range of motion. Poor flexibility is one of the biggest reasons for injury among all athletes, regardless of age and experience. Talk to your child's coach or a personal trainer to find a good flexibility program—and make sure your child uses it—routinely! Keep these tips in mind when discussing stretching with your child:

- Warm up muscles before stretching them by doing calisthenics or taking a short jog. Both increase blood flow and raise the temperature of the muscles. This makes them more pliable.

- Be sure to stretch at least five times a week.

- Stretch for at least twenty minutes, and stretch each muscle for at least thirty seconds.

- Don't bounce. Always stretch slowly and deliberately, and if you feel pain, *stop*!

- Stretch before, during, and *after* vigorous exercise to prevent tightness and soreness. Again, *stop* if you feel pain.

Six Important Principles of Weight Lifting

These principles are offered not to encourage you to organize or oversee your child's weight lifting program. Frankly, most parents are not qualified to handle such a responsibility. They are offered so that you can observe intelligently, so that you can determine if much of what your child is doing seems right. The child may lift weights at home, in school, at the community center, in the local fitness center, or elsewhere. Whatever the location, parents must be familiar with the following principles, if only to remind children of their importance.

1. *Help the child develop goals.* Having a target improves our focus, whether we're throwing a baseball, hitting a nine-iron, or lifting weights. Knowing what they want to accomplish gives kids a focus and helps them aim at something more important than looking good on the beach. When you help kids develop goals, then, be sure to help them aim at injury prevention for every part of their bodies and to focus on exercises that enhance performance for that particular sport.

Work with the coach or another training professional to identify the goals that are appropriate for your child's size, age, development, and strength levels. And be sure the child has a hand in developing the goals. When kids help develop goals, they commit to them more readily. It's easier to remind kids of the goals they set than to push them into difficult exercises they don't understand.

2. *Be sure the child warms up well.* Warming up maximizes the benefits of exercise and minimizes injuries. Children must understand that warming up and stretching are not the same thing. Warming up supplies the muscles with blood, making them more pliable. Failing to warm up before stretching can result in tears in tendons and ligaments. A warm up also avoids sudden shocks to the heart. Each child is different, but ten minutes of jogging, jumping rope, or stair climbing is usually sufficient for a warm up before lifting or other vigorous exercise.

3. *Be sure the child avoids injury.* Every child has a different tolerance for pain. One child might cry out, another only wince. Parents are in a better position than coaches to sense such problems. They know the child. In addition, some children have preexisting injuries or family predispositions to certain injuries. Parents must be sensitive to this as well, and they must help coaches be aware of them. Children can seriously injure themselves if they fail to heed the most important principle for all weight lifters: "If it hurts, *stop!*"

One summer we had a youngster on the team who wanted to be a wide receiver. Trying a bench press for the first time one day, he winced. His spotter, a teammate, called me over. I told him to stop all lifting for the rest of the day and to see the family doctor. I called home as well to let his parents know. He saw the doctor, who discovered a congenital weakness in his shoulder. It required no surgery, just a different exercise program. The boy played for us that year. What might have happened if we had pushed him that day or told him to "get tough"?

Being smart is a whole lot better than being tough. Let the pros play through pain if they want to. The money and the adulation may be worth it to them. Young athletes who play through pain risk lifelong injury. At the least, they lose important playing time. So remind them constantly, "If it hurts, *stop!*"

4. *Be sure the child wears a belt.* Weight lifting belts are available in most sports stores and are worth the investment. Lower back pain is common among most athletes, for that matter, within the general population. Rare is the adult who has never had a sore back. The small of the back is covered with small, deep muscles that are affected by the back's

larger muscles. Sometimes the smallest mistake when lifting a heavy object can result in sharp and surprisingly persistent pains.

A weight lifting belt supports and protects the small muscles that over-exertion injures so easily. Some weight lifters use a belt only when working with unusually heavy weights or when doing certain exercises that strain that area of the body. Youngsters should be encouraged to use a belt all the time. Help them develop the habit of putting it on immediately before a workout.

5. *Be sure the child breathes correctly.* Most children don't know how to breathe properly when lifting weights. They must learn that the heavier the weight, the harder the exhale. The best rule? "Inhale when you lower the weight; exhale when you lift it." In other words, "Blow through the strain!" Forced exhalation tightens the muscles, making them stronger. It also prevents excessive strain on the vascular system.

Forced exhalation also makes any motion more explosive. Many youngsters believe that holding their breath gives them more power. The opposite is true. Just watch a discus thrower or a shot putter at a track meet. They all grunt loudly at the moment of release. Listen to football players or sprinters when they come out of their stances. They all grunt to improve their explosiveness. Children, especially girls, who have the strength to engage in humane weight lifting programs may be embarrassed the first time they grunt, but they'll get used to it.

6. *Be sure the child emphasizes form over substance.* Proper form creates substance. To maximize the benefits of certain exercises, athletes must do them correctly. Doing them correctly also prevents injury.

Emphasize the following elements of form with your child:

- Don't drop the weight after lifting it, no matter what the exercise. A sudden drop of the weight can damage joints. Be deliberate. Raise and lower the weight slowly. If the weight is too heavy to raise it slowly, use less weight.

- Keep your body as straight as possible during the lift. If the weight causes you to be hunched over, you're trying to lift too much.

- Use the right amount of weight for your strength level. You're not competing with anyone but yourself.

- Set the weight on the floor or a bench between repetitions and rest for a good thirty to forty-five seconds to give your muscles enough time to recover.

- If in doubt, use less weight. If it hurts, *stop!*

Safety first. This is the key principle for any child who lifts weights. There's a right way and a wrong way to do everything, but some activities are more critical than others. If a child swings at and misses the first pitch of the game, it may be a little bothersome, but it won't have lifelong consequences for her. But if she persistently forgets to bend at the knees when lifting barbells from the floor, she's going to hurt her back and, as a middle ager, may find herself groaning every time she gets in and out of a car. That's if she's lucky. It could be a whole lot worse.

Always use a spotter. The same is true of kids who do bench presses without spotters. Spotters are athletes who help the lifter when the weights get too heavy. When doing bench presses, for example, the child may run out of strength on the last lift and be unable to get the bar up. At such times—and it has happened all too often—the weight becomes too heavy and it falls. It might land on the child's face, breaking a nose or knocking out teeth. Worse, it could land on the child's neck, suffocating him or her.

Because such injuries happen—almost every year—children should lift weights in teams of two. While one is lifting, the other spots. Alternating the exercises also gives kids some rest time between lifts. It also provides a little cheerleading during the exercise. Encouragement from a friend or teammate is very helpful during moments of strenuous exercise. Obviously, the younger the child, the better the spotter should be. Young children should have adult spotters.

The Most Important Point. More important than any of this, however, is the fact that lifting weights may be too demanding for many young athletes. This point can't be overemphasized. Most youngsters' joints haven't matured enough to handle the strain of lifting weights, particularly given their desire to try to lift too much. One thoughtless moment with a barbell can have long-lasting consequences. Nothing in a child's life is important enough to risk lifelong disability.

Those of you who played sports, even recreational tennis or golf, understand the consequences of pushing your body beyond its limits. Sometimes the injuries we cause don't act up until later in life, and then we wonder if it was all worth it. I think I'd probably play football again, but I'm not sure, especially when I wince in pain every time I put my socks on or get out of my chair.

Aerobic Training: Why?

The answer is simple. Every athlete in every sport requires cardiovascular efficiency. Even short-burst activities like sprinting and football require oxygen. Recognize, however, that oxygen itself does not supply energy to muscles. Simple and complex carbohydrates, transformed into glycogen, are the big suppliers of energy. So is fat, but oxygen is required to release it. Aerobic training, therefore, is essential if athletes are to improve their performance, including their endurance.

The heart of a well-conditioned athlete may beat fifty to sixty times per minute, sometimes as low as forty. This means that the athlete's heart, when compared to the average person's, may beat thirteen million fewer times each year.

Aerobic means "with oxygen." It is the oxygen in the blood that releases energy and burns fat. So make sure your child is taking in sufficient oxygen during exercise to burn fat. If he or she can talk or whistle while jogging, the exercise is about right. Pushing harder and believing such silliness as "no pain, no gain" creates "anaerobic" exercise ("without oxygen") that fails to build aerobic endurance, burn fat, and improve appearance.

Let's be realistic. Parents must be sure, however, not to lose sight of the fact that most kids have enough energy to power a nuclear sub. Their levels of activity and their youth guarantee most kids good aerobic training, so they don't need rigorous running or jogging programs. In addition, the intensity of competition and the physical demands of most sports for seven- and eight-year-olds are considerably less than for high school athletes. A few laps after practice every other day or even once a week are enough for most kids.

This is not true for kids in high school. Competition for them is intense, and the physical demands on their bodies are more pronounced. Aerobic efficiency is critical for them, so parents can expect coaches to run kids enough to build up their cardiovascular systems. Most will emphasize both aerobic and anaerobic exercises to assure their athletes the conditioning levels they need to compete successfully.

So once again, it's a matter of developmental levels. Youngsters don't need the same weight training and cardiovascular programs required of older athletes, and, even if the athlete is older, all he or she needs is a humane and consistent program that develops aerobic endurance. So, parents, make sure the child, no matter what age, doesn't overdo.

But celebrate the fact that the child is learning self-discipline. Too many kids these days get their exercise flying off the handle, bending the rules, dodging responsibility, passing the buck, beating the system, or pushing their luck. A humane weight training program enhances performance, prevents injuries, builds self-confidence, and creates self-discipline.

Make sure the child drinks water—lots of it. Athletes must replace body fluids—frequently—while competing, practicing, or watching TV. We are all approximately 60 percent water; even a loss of 10 percent of that water can lead to heat stroke. Kids must drink at least eight ounces of water for every ten minutes of vigorous exercise. Parents and coaches must be sure, therefore, to provide ample water for kids, especially on hot days.

A loss of only 5 percent of the body's water can lead to headaches, weakness, and rapid pulse—all symptoms of heat exhaustion. It can also lead to diminished mental capacity, the depletion of blood cells, the buildup of toxins in the body, less oxygen to the muscles, and reduced perspiration, the body's cooling mechanism.

Many young wrestlers, for example, stop drinking water to lose weight before weigh-ins. The tactic works. They lose weight, but the loss is only temporary. After the match, when they load up on water, they put the weight back on and have to do it all over again for the next weigh-in. Worse, the absence of water causes a light dose of heat exhaustion, which causes listlessness and slight nausea. Listless and nauseated wrestlers don't win many matches.

C.U.B.S.

To help young athletes maintain energy levels and avoid cramping and fatigue, teach them the word C.U.B.S to remind them to drink lots of water:

C—Cells. The cells in the human body require a lot of water to do what they have to do.

U—Urination. Urination eliminates toxic substances from the body.

B—Blood. By drinking water, athletes increase the volume of blood in their bodies. This increased volume brings more oxygen to their brains and muscles.

S—Sweat. Water causes perspiration, which cools the body.

Let's Wrap It Up

I coached for thirty-one years, trying within that time to win as many games as I could. Looking back on it all, I'm proud to say that the most important focus of this chapter has *not* been on conditioning and its contribution to a winning program. To the contrary, my experience has taught me that winning is a whole lot less important than assuring that kids are safe and that they have fun. Conditioning is important, primarily because it prevents injuries.

But, a poorly organized conditioning program can itself cause injuries. So the most important points in this chapter have been: "Don't overdo" and "If it hurts, *stop!*" Conditioning programs for young athletes, even in high school, need not be as rigorous as for professional or elite athletes. Young kids and professionals both may be trying to win, but their purposes are different. Professionals are making a very good living by continuing to compete with pulled muscles and broken bones.

But, it's no intellectual stretch to realize that such behaviors *aren't fun!* Kids want to have fun, and no one blames them. So let's keep the conditioning program in perspective. Any actual competition may involve a sense of urgency, the kind that pushes athletes, no matter what the age, to make a maximum effort. The conditioning program, however, especially for kids, doesn't involve the same level of intensity. In fact, any "hurry-up" approach to conditioning simply doesn't work.

Conditioning, even aerobic training, requires a slow, deliberate focus on form. Children who run too fast don't burn fat or improve their appearance or fitness levels. Kids who disregard proper nutrition and eat too much slow themselves down and lose mobility and quickness. And kids who lift too much weight can't use proper form. As a result, they fail to increase muscle mass and to strengthen key areas of the body that could be susceptible to injury.

As with everything else in life, kids have to learn to "let moderation prevail." Most parents have learned that sometimes the faster we go, the further we fall behind. Kids must learn the same lesson. They must work hard at conditioning, especially to prevent injury, but they must do it slowly and deliberately. And, above all, they must have fun. Elite athletes expect pain when they practice and compete. Kids, however, lose interest when the pain of preparing exceeds the pleasures of playing. We can't let that happen.

4.
INJURY AND
THE YOUNG ATHLETE

Did You Know?

- Almost 1.5 million high school athletes are injured every year.

- Children from five to fourteen years of age incur one-third of all sports injuries.

- An estimated one-third of all high school football players are sidelined because of injury every year.

- Almost 25 percent of all girls playing high school basketball miss one or more games because of injury.

Competition has become so intense, even in youth sports, that injury is almost a way of life for many athletes. Unfortunately, not even the best conditioning program can prevent some of them. Interestingly, one of the reasons for this increase in injuries is the immoderate behavior of adult athletes. Our tendency to overdo an exercise regimen causes us a lot of unnecessary pain, and we are modeling the same well-intentioned excesses for our kids.

Look Out for Overuse Injuries
Athletic participation and competition have become so widespread in our society that many kids are now playing some sports year round. Most have

been convinced by parents and coaches that a year-round focus is necessary for success. Others have been influenced by the glamour and excitement of professional and Olympic sports.

An orthopedic clinic that opened in the mid-70s reported that up to 80 percent of the sports injuries then were traumatic. Today, most of the injuries are the result of joint and muscle overuse.

Kids watch all this and either commit themselves to or are pushed into year-round, intensive programs that make demands not only on their time, but their bodies. Years ago, children did not incur stress fractures in growth plates or develop "Little League elbow." Tendonitis and shin splints were the purview of those of us who, as young adults, played the sports we loved in high school and college. Kids never suffered such acute and persistent injuries.

Seven Physical Factors That Lead to Injury

What then are the specifics that parents must understand to prevent such problems for their children? The following seven important factors identify problems not only with competitive but with recreational sports. Both must be watched carefully by parents:

1. *Slow reaction time.* Because they are still growing, most youngsters don't have the coordination or reaction time of older athletes or adults.

While watching a Pop Warner football game a few years ago, I was struck by something peculiar about the game but couldn't put my finger on it. Suddenly, a parent approached me and said, "Don't they look like they're playing in slow motion?" That was it.

2. *Different levels of maturation.* Children competing in Little League or Pop Warner programs come in all sizes and shapes. If coaches fail to accommodate smaller or less coordinated children in drills or contests, children will be overmatched. One result for such children is injury, another is the decision to quit the sport.

3. *Size and strength in older children.* As beneficial as conditioning programs are to performance and injury prevention for most athletes, they have resulted in bigger, stronger kids in junior high and high school who overpower smaller, less well-conditioned opponents. This is as true for neighborhood pickup games as it is for Pop Warner and Little League contests.

Studies show that in a recent decade, 72 percent of the players in the NFL suffered injuries that kept them sidelined for up to eight weeks. Worse, the percentage of players who suffered career-ending injuries has doubled since the 1950s.

4. *Failure to condition the entire body.* This disparity in size and strength is yet another reason for parents to make sure that their children condition their entire bodies, not just the muscles that look good on the beach. Coaches, because they know the parts of the body that are particularly susceptible to injury in

their sports, must also engage kids in lifting and conditioning programs that strengthen key areas of each athlete's body. Failure to do so can result in unnecessary injury for lots of kids.

As indicated in one of my earlier books, Building the Total Athlete, "Some orthopedic surgeons have gone so far as to indicate that loose-jointed youngsters should avoid contact sports like football, lacrosse, and field hockey—and that tight-jointed athletes should avoid running and swimming activities."

Young athletes who are seriously committed to a single sport and tend to overuse certain muscle groups must be reminded often to warm up and stretch before practice or competition. Failure to warm up muscles is one of the most serious problems for all athletes, no matter what age, but it is especially important for youngsters who are dedicated to a single sport.

5. *Poor fitness levels.* Many poorly conditioned youngsters insist on playing rigorously competitive sports. Careless training techniques and a short-sighted approach to strenuous competition cause problems for thousands of kids every year. Again, if the child is unwilling to commit to an effective training program, parents must *just say no* to his or her desire to compete.

Coaches must also say *no* to the temptation to drill skills into players to the point of exhaustion or serious overuse of parts of the body. Repetition of both fundamental and advanced skills is essential if youngsters are to perform them routinely. Excessive drill time, however, can seriously damage growth plates in youngsters and previously injured or weak joints in more mature athletes. In addition, research indicates that athletes learn a lot from the first ten minutes of a drill and less from the second ten minutes.

In essence, young pitchers will learn a great deal from the first twenty-five curve balls they throw in practice, much less from the next twenty-five. The key for good coaches, therefore, is to schedule shorter drill segments. The baseball coach should schedule a ten-minute segment for throwing curve balls, a second ten-minute segment for fielding ground balls, then a third ten-minute segment for throwing curve balls again. The children will learn more about throwing curve balls, and the rest they receive between pitching segments will prevent overuse of selected muscle groups.

6. *Poor fundamental skills.* Let's admit it, many youth program coaches are well-intentioned, but don't have the knowledge or the background to teach fundamental skills to most of the kids on their teams. Consider just the demand of most coaches to "bull the neck" when blocking or tackling in football. A bulled neck uses the muscle pad in the back of the neck to cushion the head. It's that simple. Any tendency to "align the spine," to forget to bull the neck, results in a failure to provide this cushion the head needs for protection. This simple mistake can result in disability or death.

My football career ended because of a cerebral hemorrhage. All I did was drop my head on one play. I made one error in fundamentals, and it almost cost me my life.

Certainly, the failure to teach fundamental skills won't always result in such dramatic consequences. But any failure to teach young athletes how to rotate the upper body to throw a football or a baseball, how to slide into second base, or how to shuffle the feet correctly when playing defense in basketball can result in shoulder injuries or twisted ankles for many kids. This is one reason why communities should require coaches not only to learn first aid but to master as much as possible about their sports before being allowed to work with youngsters.

This knowledge will also help coaches assure that kids are using the right equipment. For example, well-cushioned shoes are critical for young runners, tennis, volleyball, and basketball players; a proper fitting helmet is a must for young football and hockey players; and well-fitting shoes are essential for young soccer and field hockey players. Parents need not get involved in fitting the equipment, but an occasional question such as "How's that helmet feel?" or "Shoes comfortable?" will assure you that the equipment is fine. ·

7. *Failure to recognize the unique needs of girls.* Girls and women have come a long way in sports, and they have proven their courage, commitment, and skill levels. Many of the finest athletes in the world are women. But, compared to males, females have unique needs that parents and coaches must recognize. Ongoing and vigorous training can cause some females to lose their menstrual cycles which can result in brittle bones and stress fractures.

Doctors at a New York hospital also indicate that, although men's and women's injuries are similar, women may suffer more musculoskeletal disorders than men. In addition, knee and abdominal injuries may be more pronounced. Parents and coaches are well-advised, therefore, to be sensitive to such possibilities and to provide training experiences that prevent such potential problems for female athletes.

Six Psychological Factors That Lead to Injury

Athletes of all ages are predisposed to injury for a variety of psychological reasons. Because parents are the front line of defense against such problems, they should be familiar with certain behaviors that predispose their kids to injury. Because some of these behaviors are very subtle, parents and coaches must be willing to take the time to look carefully at the puzzling and sometimes frustrating behaviors of young athletes. Parents should be especially alert to the following traits in their children:

1. *Tendency to take risks.* Kids take risks for a variety of reasons. Some are unfamiliar with the consequences of their behavior. Many are overconfident, while a surprisingly large number are *under*confident. Overconfident youngsters leap into the fray with little thought for their safety, certain that they can handle anything that comes their way. Underconfident kids do things because they feel they have to.

Young football players, for example, will throw themselves carelessly at bigger opponents to prove their courage to teammates or coaches. Injury is likely for both children, but especially for the underconfident child because he is likely to disregard safety in a mad dash to prove himself to others and probably to himself.

2. *Doing things they shouldn't do.* "Be tough" has echoed in gymnasiums and playing fields for as long as coaches have worn whistles. As far back as any

of us can remember, athletes of all ages have been expected to play with pain for the good of the team. Playing with pain was also another opportunity to prove how tough you are. It goes without saying that athletes who play injured are subject to further injury. Their mobility and flexibility are limited. Even if they don't make the original injury worse, they're likely to be injured somewhere else.

We had a defensive tackle one year who used to get a lot of "stingers," pinched nerves in his neck. Because they're so painful, they're very limiting. Our big concern was the player's pain tolerance. When he got a stinger, he'd just flinch briefly, then get back into the huddle. We learned to recognize "the flinch" in order to pull him out of practice and have him stand next to us until the pain subsided.

Kids have different pain tolerances. Parents and coaches must recognize this in their children and keep an eye out for the "flinchers." More important, they should discuss potential injury with kids *beforehand* to make sure they understand the consequences of playing with pain. Trying their best to be tough, to prove their invulnerability, young athletes who play with pain expect to give 110 percent. They're disappointed and disillusioned when they discover that they can give only 50 percent. This disparity of effort and output compels them to try even harder—a fact that almost always leads to more injury.

3. *Being afraid to lose a starting position.* Insecure athletes and youngsters who are barely hanging on to starting positions or a place on the team often ignore pain in order to keep playing. Consider baseball's Iron Man, Lou Gehrig. A utility infielder for the New York Yankees back in the '20s, Gehrig got the starting position at first base for the Yanks in 1925, when the

starter, Wally Pipp, got injured. Pipp was a good player, but we didn't hear much from him again. Gehrig went on to start 2,130 games in succession, the longest string in history until Cal Ripken broke the record in 1995.

No young athlete worth his or her salt wants to be "Wally Pipped." Youngsters join sports team to play, and they want to play as much as they can. Their love of the game is just one reason. Being a starter gives kids status. Adults can identify with that. We all want to be "players." And as parents, we all want our kids to be players, so many of us, perhaps inadvertently, are among the forces that pressure kids to play hurt. All parents should be especially careful of this tendency.

4. *Experiencing considerable stress in their lives.* Interestingly, one of the biggest causes of injury to many athletes is the amount of life stress they experience prior to or during competition. Normal amounts of stress are to be expected, especially before and during competition. This kind of stress is normally good because it motivates kids to do their best. The bad stress, the kind that leads to injuries— especially for young athletes—is the pressure that results from changing schools, experiencing divorce or separation in the family, or losing a family member.

When young athletes are confronted with such significant stresses in their lives, parents must provide consistent support for them to avoid injury. They also should alert the coach. Involvement in athletics may be exactly what kids need at such times in their lives, but they might also need time away from the sport to make needed adjustments. When young athletes become preoccupied with the circumstances of their lives, they fail to focus on practice or game situations, lose interest in conditioning and important nutritional habits, minimize dangerous situations, and develop an "I don't care" attitude that affects their performance and subjects them to injury.

5. *Imagining, fabricating, or inviting injury.* Self-deception affects athletes as much as anyone else in our society. Consciously trying to play their best, some athletes will unconsciously imagine or invite injury. This happens for several reasons. Some youngsters, deep down, either don't like the game or are afraid to play it. They may have been pushed into competition and feel that an injury is an excusable way out. Such children need support and, if necessary, permission to find an activity that is more to their liking.

Other kids may be angry at coaches or parents for being pushed too hard and may actually invite injury to "get even." In essence, the child endures pain in order to provoke guilt in the adult. In other instances, when children are convinced that they can't do what is expected, an injury will permit them to stop trying. Then there's the child with poor self-esteem who is unable to accept recent success and invites injury so that his or her coaches and parents stop expecting more success.

Each of these children requires similar treatment. They all need a supportive, understanding approach that puts athletic competition in perspective for them and for others. Pressure to perform works insidiously on different kids. Some love the challenge and respond by excelling. Others fear the challenge and respond by experiencing real or imaginary injuries. Others quit, claiming that it wasn't fun. And they're probably right.

6. *Wanting to be one-sport athletes.* Young athletes are being pressured more and more every year to concentrate only on one sport. The primary reason usually involves the desire of the coach and/or parents to focus on the specific skills the athlete must have to excel in the sport. At one extreme, some young boys and girls who want to compete at elite or professional levels are leaving their families to live with coaches in order to develop their gymnastics, tennis, or swimming skills. Such athletes are very talented youngsters who share a willingness with their parents to sacrifice much of their youth in pursuit of their athletic goals.

Other athletes have interests and skills that project success for them in certain sports. Based on body type and talent levels, some youngsters tend to focus on basketball, volleyball, softball, football, or other sports suited to their ability levels. These young athletes may not seek elite or professional futures, but they're probably thinking about athletic scholarships to college.

My little 8-year-old neighbor just loves baseball. I saw him a couple weeks ago out on the street with a bat and ball. He said, "Hey, Doc, (the kids call me Doc) watch this. I'm the greatest hitter in the world." With that, he threw the ball in the air, swung his bat, and missed the ball. Shouting once more "I'm the greatest hitter in the world," he threw the ball and again missed it. The same thing happened a third time. Finally he looked at me and said, "You know, maybe I'm not the greatest hitter in the world. I'm the greatest pitcher!"

The point is, single-sport athletes—regardless of their self-confidence, aspirations, self-assessments, and ability to adjust in mid-stream—tend to overuse specific muscle groups and to risk aches and pains for the rest of their lives. Parents and coaches are well-advised to encourage their children to play more than one sport or, at least, to put that sport in perspective and to do everything necessary to avoid overuse injuries.

The Five Stages of the Young Athlete's Reaction to Injury

All athletes, no matter what age, react differently to injury. A few welcome the injury as an excuse to miss practice. These kids are usually on the field or court for something other than love of the game. For most athletes, injury is a serious challenge to their expectations for the season, their self-concepts, even their goals for the future. Dedicated athletes hate the thought of missing one or more contests. Worse yet, they may fear the loss of their playing careers.

When the doctors at Nebraska told me that the cerebral hemorrhage ended my playing career, I was shocked, even immobilized for several weeks. I had already been told that several pro teams had been interested in me. I even had an offer to play in Canada before I transferred to Nebraska. The loss was painful. At the banquet at the end of the season, I was even reluctant to pick up my award, feeling I hadn't earned it.

Even the threat of a career-ending injury is a substantial loss to all athletes, not just the highly talented. Gifted athletes may fear the loss of scholarships or professional futures, but all athletes, even the least gifted, fear the loss of an activity that helped form their self-concept, provided security, and formed important friendships. Fortunately, the loss provoked by injury affects them in predictable ways. Parents must be the first to understand the stages kids go through when injury forces them to miss competition or end a career.

Psychologists report that an athlete's reaction to injury is similar to the stages people go through when dying. This may sound a bit extreme to most parents, especially to those of you who regard your child's sport as just a game. But this doesn't deny the importance of that game to your child. The loss is still extremely upsetting to athletes, even young athletes. Parents must be familiar with these five stages:

1. *Denial and isolation.* Sudden and debilitating injury can be so unexpected that it comes as a shock. It did to me. Athletes invariably respond by asserting, "Not me! This did *not* happen to me!" Then, they usually deny the seriousness of the injury: "I'll shake this off and be back next week." Finally, they feel alone, shut off from the rest of the team, almost outcast because of their inability to contribute.

2. *Anger.* Denial is normally followed by anger, especially when they discover the consequences of the injury. Their anger makes them ask questions like, "Why me?" or "How could this have happened to me?" They are easily irritated, even to the point of refusing treatment or advice.

3. *Bargaining.* Gradually beginning to accept the implications of the injury, athletes ask, "If I'm good, can I get better? If I work hard at rehab, can I be as good as ever?" Bargaining usually signals the start of a general acceptance of the injury but still leads to stage four.

4. *Depression.* Stage four involves the inevitable depression that follows anger. Any kind of depression is usually the result of unexpressed or unresolved anger. People who are angry at the circumstances of their lives and—for whatever reason—are unable to resolve the anger can become immobilized by it. Saying and thinking, "What's the use?" they are unable to find the energy to fight back. This stage requires considerable support from parents and coaches. If the athlete simply gives up, rehabilitation is compromised, and the return to competition is delayed further.

5. *Acceptance or resignation.* It is at this stage that athletes ask, "Okay, what now?" They have accepted the injury for what it is and are willing to do whatever is necessary to repair it or to get on with the rest of their lives.

Parents and coaches must understand these five stages because they go well beyond traditional ways of dealing with injured athletes, even very young ones. Tradition allowed coaches to shame kids into returning to competition, implying that they weren't tough or were letting the team down. Coaches genuinely believed—some still do—that a failure to "get tough" with injured athletes prolonged their rehabilitation and allowed them to "go soft." What could be worse for young kids?

These kinds of traditions fail to understand that most kids have to be prepared psychologically to return to competition, that their fears of re-injury are real. Even when trainers and doctors tell kids that they're ready to return to competition, some don't *feel* ready, and this is true of even older athletes. The memory of pain and debility are still too vivid in their minds. Having been proven vulnerable by the injury, they fear further injury, particularly if they return to competition too soon.

Many of us tend to look at athletes as being special, and they are. I told all my players repeatedly that they were special. Not that many kids are willing to give up a quick trip to the shopping mall after school in order to exhaust themselves during drills and scrimmages, then run wind sprints before going home to an evening of homework. But it's important for us—and for all those coaches out there—to remember that athletes may be willing to abuse their bodies more than the average bear, but that they're still *human.*

I may have been able to push my face into an opponent's body to keep him away from the quarterback, but I sure didn't enjoy getting hurt. And when I was hurt, I didn't *enjoy* having my coach belittle me for not playing. I may have enjoyed running into my fellow man, but I was smart enough to see through such coaching tactics, even to distrust people who used them. Injuries are forgotten sooner than insults. This is true in every walk of life. Parents and coaches must understand that dealing with injury requires substantially different treatment if kids are to return to competition to help their teams and to enjoy the sports they love.

Five Bad Reactions and What Parents Can Do to Help

Injury affects the self-image of most athletes. Even young athletes, particularly if they compete for a few years, identify strongly with their sports, often to the point of being inseparable from them. It isn't rare, for example, for a boy to think of himself as "Tom, the football player" or for a girl to think of herself as "Jill, the soccer player." I guess many of us would prefer that these two kids think of themselves as school valedictorians, but that's pretty restricted company, so let's allow them to capitalize on *their* strengths.

Too strong an identification with a sport, of course, is not good either. We want our children's interests and aspirations to be varied, just as we want them to find success in different areas. But even the most multitalented children, especially if injured during the season, experience a sudden loss of competition that angers and depresses them. The loss also affects a powerful element of their self-image and provokes several, maybe all five, stages of reaction to the injury. At such times, many kids are unable to think clearly about the injury and its implications for them.

In an article titled "Cognitive Therapy" (1970), A. T. Beck identified five irrational ways many athletes may react to the anxiety and damaged self-concept caused by injury. Parents are encouraged to watch their children carefully to see if they:

1. *Exaggerate the meaning of the injury.* This can range from, "Oh, it's nothing; I'll be all right," to, "It looks like my season's over," or, "I guess I'll never play again." Remember, such reactions may seem extreme to adults, but probably reflect the natural impulsivity of most kids. No matter which extreme the athlete may take, parents are well-advised to help them focus on the facts of the injury and emphasize the short-term realities as opposed to the long-term possibilities.

2. *Disregard aspects of injury.* The desire to get back to competition as quickly as possible can frustrate kids. Informed by a trainer or the family doctor that rehab will take two to three weeks, some kids

will get frustrated after one week and start making demands to rejoin the team as soon as possible. Such disregard for the importance of rehab can have long-term implications if parents give in. If reason doesn't work, this is another time to "Just say no."

3. *Oversimplify the injury.* If that hairline fracture on a rib could turn into a compound break and puncture a lung, the implications of the injury cannot be oversimplified. An injury is not just good or bad. It's much more complicated than that. That's why this is the time to sit the child down with the family doctor and explain all the implications of the injury, not to load him down with scare tactics but to get his eyes open to its realities.

4. *Over-generalize.* Some athletes will compare their injuries to the injuries of other athletes who never fully recovered. Such overgeneralizations can cause athletes, especially very young ones, to back away from rehab or to be more anxious about the implications of the injury. At such times, parents must remind them of the many athletes who *have* fully recovered from such injuries and *why* they recovered.

5. *Make unwarranted conclusions.* An injury, especially if it is moderately serious, can lead kids into unwarranted assumptions. Some may conclude that their conditioning was useless and back away from additional conditioning. Some may blame coaches or other athletes for their problems. Some may even start to believe that they are injury prone and return to competition with a hesitancy that surely will lead to further injury.

How to Help Injured Athletes

Parents must understand and be able to recognize these reactions to injury. The message is clear. Injury causes children to suffer psychological as well as physical pain. It is this psychological pain that can cause youngsters—and older athletes—to experience a depression that colors their entire lives, to minimize the importance of rehabilitation, to feel less confident in their ability to compete successfully, and to consciously or unconsciously worry about re-injury. These reactions of athletes haven't been fabricated in a research report for their dramatic value. They may be subtle, and children may try valiantly to hide them, but they are very real.

Parents must be able to recognize them and to help their children overcome them by responding in very specific ways. Fortunately, we don't need a Ph.D. in psychology to reach out to an injured child, just the willingness to provide support. Reasonable support and a willingness to listen are at the core of what is needed. Such support is not a do-gooders call to action. In fact, a too sympathetic response to an injured child may rob him or her of the psychological strength to do everything that is necessary to overcome the injury.

The following are a few suggestions for parents. When your child is recovering from an injury:

Help your child and others understand the injury. The child must be told if the injury is serious. If it can be rehabilitated effectively, the child must be told how long it will take and what to do to help the healing. Then he or she must be given the support to do all that is necessary to rehab it successfully. In addition, parents must aggressively share their doctor's diagnosis of the injury and his or her rehabilitation plans with the child's coach. When sharing such information, parents must take the time to emphasize with coaches the importance of the psychological aspects of rehabilitation. All of us who care about kids and the world of sports must do everything we can to combat the traditional "get tough" approaches of too many coaches.

Reassure the child and provide support whenever necessary. This does not mean that parents must commiserate and sympathize with their injured children. In fact, sometimes it means that parents will have to stand firm in their expectations that children can tolerate the pain and inconvenience of ongoing rehabilitation. While doing so, however, parents must empathize with the child and congratulate him or her on having the willingness and courage to do something that is obviously so difficult. As indicated throughout this chapter, the process involves an awareness of both the physical *and* the psychological implications of the injury.

Years ago, we had a young fullback who inhaled and ingested an almost fatal dose of gasoline siphoning gas from a truck while working with his dad on a construction site. His doctors were convinced that he would never play football again, but the constant support of family and teammates proved them wrong. He began running, almost always with three or more teammates, and showed up on the first day of practice—good as new. Dubbed "Motor Man" by his coach, he became an all-conference fullback and became an inspiration to everyone in the community.

Help him or her focus on the current treatment plan. All of us, especially children, may expect the worst when adversity comes our way. The shock of a sudden injury can conjure up all kinds of dire circumstances for kids. Our job as parents and coaches is to help them refocus their energies on the here and now, to stick to the treatment plan and to trust that complete rehabilitation is possible. It doesn't matter whether athletes are preparing for a game or recovering from an injury. Both require positive self-talk, a belief in themselves, and the awareness that teammates, coaches, and parents support them.

Help the child put the injury in perspective. In most instances, an injury is not the end of a journey. Help the child put it into controllable units and deal with each of them at the right time. In addition, injury represents a remarkable opportunity for kids to learn how to focus their attention on *all* their responsibilities—at home, at school , as well as in the rehab room.

I learned a very successful strategy years ago. When my athletes were injured or victimized by an unfortunate turn of events in their lives, I helped them realize the importance of dealing with such problems head on. But they also had to learn to put the original problem in a box, close the lid, and postpone dealing with it when other important responsibilities in their lives required their attention.

This is a difficult thing for many kids to do, just as it is for you and me. But this is what adults do, and it's something that kids must learn. Life is a mosaic of different responsibilities, each of which requires our full attention. School homework and studies, family relationships and chores, the needs of friends, preparation for entrance into high school or college, and a whole range of other responsibilities require the time and attention of injured athletes. Help children to focus attention on injuries when appropriate, but to give equal attention to other responsibilities when necessary.

When to Return to Competition

Young athletes must be helped to maintain as many normal contacts as possible during the recovery period. The return of the young fullback in the earlier story from what might have been a lifelong disability was made possible by his family and the coaches and teammates who stood by him. Without the motivation they provided, he may have recovered anyway. He was a tough kid. But there is no doubt in my mind that they helped more than anyone will ever know. Even his doctors indicated that his friends and family turned the tide by sharing the healing power of love.

Just about everyone in the medical community now accepts the fact that the mind and the body work together. It's important for us to acknowledge, therefore, that the physical and the psychological aspects of an injury are inseparable from each other. On that basis, parents and coaches must remember to provide not only the rehabilitation program needed by injured athletes, but also the emotional support kids need to recover from a painful injury and to return to competition.

Recovering from an injury involves much more than healed tissues and strengthened joints. Young athletes will also need help dealing with a possible inability to display their former talents, an unwillingness to accept new but temporary limitations, or the reality that re-injury is possible. Be sure, then, to get an okay from the family doctor for the physical side, but respond to the psychological side as well by talking with the child and providing support and advice wherever possible.

Warm up and stretch! When the child does return to competition, make sure he or she warms up and stretches the injured area before vigorous exercise and competition. Previous injuries often remain tight and require more than the usual amount of blood flow to achieve a full range of motion. Also encourage the child to pace himself or herself. Nothing causes re-injury faster than sudden, explosive movement. Even the toughest athletes baby themselves a little. A slower pace is a whole lot better than a painful return to the original injury.

A Few Final Words

Parents, particularly of young athletes, are among the first to respond to minor injuries. It's important for them to understand the difference between fatigue and injury. If your child complains of distress after practice or competition, be sure to observe him or her to get answers to the following questions:

Is the pain symmetrical? Is it found only in one part of the body? Is it found in one quadraceps and not the other, one hamstring and not the other?

Is it immediate? Does the pain recur as soon as the child moves a certain way or does a certain exercise?

Does the pain persist? Muscular fatigue should gradually disappear. It should not recur when exercise resumes or during periods of rest.

Be sure to answer these questions as soon as the child complains of pain. See the family doctor if the pain persists or intensifies.

Sometimes, however, kids come home from practice or competition with injuries that don't require immediate medical treatment: slight twists, contusions, sore muscles. Always be aware that such aches and pains may indicate something more serious, but usually all they require is a little TLC and some quick treatment from mom or dad.

Keep the acronym RICE in mind when providing such treatment:

- *R*est. Give the injury some time to heal itself. The best way to do that is to rest the joint or the muscle for an extended period of time.

- *I*ce. Ice has been an important part of the treatment of injuries for many years. It slows down swelling and promotes healing. When my daughters were involved in track and basketball, I always filled Styrofoam cups with water and froze them. When one of them needed to ice an injury or a sore muscle, my wife or I took one from the freezer and broke off the top edges of the cup to reveal the ice. Then we had them hold the bottom of the cup and run the ice across the injured area for up to fifteen or more minutes. We were always careful, however, to use the ice on bare skin for only very short periods of time, if at all. In the interest of safety, it's probably best to use some kind of cloth barrier when applying ice.

- *Compression*. As effective as ice is for the treatment of injury, it is even more effective when applied along with pressure. The combination of the two can reduce swelling by as much as 80 percent. A study at Penn

State University, for example, found that using ice under a wrap reduced swelling by up to 33 percent. Ice applied *over* a compression bandage, however, reduced it by 75 percent. Obviously, such treatment is most effective when used as soon as possible after the injury.

- *Elevation.* While resting or icing the injury, be sure to keep it elevated. This, too, decreases blood flow and inhibits swelling.

More important than all this is to recognize that pain is a signal, maybe a very important one, that something is wrong. Usually, kids get minor aches and pains when competing in sports, but sometimes that nagging ache, especially in a youngster with a high tolerance for pain, signals something more serious. When in doubt, contact the family doctor. As indicated early in this chapter, kids are more susceptible than adults to stress fractures and joint injuries.

In an article "The Bare Bones of Preventing Sports Injuries" on parentsoup.com, Dr. Matthew Matava reminds parents to protect kids from overuse injuries. Says Matava, "That doesn't mean keeping them away from sports. It does mean remembering that a child's growing cartilage tissue is relatively softer than adult cartilage, making it at greater risk for injury."

To prevent injury in young athletes, parents and coaches are well-advised to remember that children in sports are not lower case versions of college or professional athletes. The rules and expectations that apply to older athletes are not appropriate for kids, not even for most high school athletes. Secondary school athletes may not be quite as susceptible as younger kids to certain kinds of injuries, but they're still developing, too.

The other day I saw a teenager come into the fitness center wearing a T-shirt that made me smile. On the front was printed "Bear with me" and on the back it read, "God hasn't finished with me." As he walked by me, I said, "In more ways than one, huh?" He smiled, muttered a "Yep," and sauntered into the weight room, ready to muscle up and take on the world.

Let's Wrap It Up

This brings up another important point, and this is not a shocker to most parents. Sometimes our most important job is to protect kids from themselves. Most kids don't consider their limitations. Sometimes this is good.

On the way out to practice one day, one of my running backs sidled up next to me and said, "Hey, Doc, no one is going to tackle me today in the scrimmage." I said, "That's a pretty big order, Tom. You mean the entire scrimmage?" He said, "Yeah," and loped ahead of me. Well, he did get tackled in the scrimmage—often. But after about twenty minutes, he broke away for a long touchdown run. When he jogged back from the run, he tossed the ball to me and said, "See, I told you!"

I like that story. I used it in an earlier book, *Coaching Character* (Sorin Books). Sometimes the refusal to accept our limitations works miracles. Unfortunately, at other times it doesn't. A high potential for stress fractures, cartilage tears, and other problems caused by the overuse of growing joints can result not only in loss of playing time but in lifelong discomfort. Sometimes the refusal to accept our limitations can result in other problems as well.

A friend of mine, a girls' field hockey coach, tells the story of a young athlete who had severe asthma but insisted on showing how tough she was by not using her inhaler. Early in the year, my friend could hear her wheezing at the far end of the field and would shout at her to sit down, relax a minute, and use her inhaler. After doing this several times, she eventually took the girl aside and told her, "Honey, either you use your inhaler regularly, or you're done on this team." Expecting to be congratulated for her toughness, the girl was shocked—but she started using her inhaler.

Saying something like this to a dedicated young athlete is difficult. Coaches routinely try to reward commitment. But coaches and parents cannot permit kids to endanger themselves for the good of the team or to prove how tough they are.

Nor can we endanger them by imposing big league expectations on Little League kids. My grandson is nine and a gifted young athlete. (Can I say otherwise?) His Little League coach wanted him to pitch as well as play second base. My son-in-law, a personal fitness trainer, told the coach no, indicating that he wouldn't allow that kind of strain on his son's joints.

Fortunately, Eric's dad understands the potential problems that result from the overuse of developing joints. Most of us don't have the same knowledge. This is not to say that no kids should pitch in Little League games. But if they do, coaches must assure that they will have sufficient rest between pitching assignments and that they pitch no more than five or six innings a week. Anything other than that suggests that winning is more important than the well-being of young athletes.

Finally, as I look back on the injury that ended my football career, I wonder about my own willingness to relive the moment. Knowing what I know now and having suffered through the excesses of my youth, would I do it all over again? Would I risk a cerebral hemorrhage to play football? Absolutely not. Were I twenty-one again and caught up in the tradition, challenge, and excitement of the game I loved, would I risk a future brain injury to enjoy the immediate fascination of picking up a critical first down in the most important game of the season? Maybe. Probably.

Sobering thought, isn't it? Your kids, no matter how young they are, might be willing to risk the same things. Keep an eye on them.

5.
THE YOUNG ATHLETE
AND BURNOUT

Did You Know?

- Athletes of any age can experience significant depression after a big victory.

- Many high school and college athletes spend more time on basketball than their professional counterparts.

- Visualizing an athletic skill activates the athlete's nerve endings and provides almost the same advantages as practicing the skill physically.

- Coaches and parents who constantly criticize and find fault increase the incidence of burnout among all athletes.

Let's start with a quick reminder that more than 50 percent of kids quit sports before their teens. Obviously, many more quit during their teens and later. Most of them are burned out. Burned out at age nine? Age has little to do with burnout. The accepted definition of burnout is "worn out or exhausted, especially from long-term stress."

My experience as both an athlete and a coach taught me that athletes can get worn out or exhausted, even on a short-term basis. Very young athletes with limited exposure to a sport experience the same stress and monotonous repetition as college and professional athletes. The problems may be even worse for very young athletes because their coaches, unlike their college and professional counterparts, are unfamiliar with the signs of burnout and the principles and strategies that prevent it.

This chapter considers many of those strategies and principles. As important as burnout prevention may be, equally important for parents is the knowledge of the characteristics in young athletes that can lead to burnout and the ability to recognize the behaviors that signal its onset. Parents must understand how to deal with these behaviors in order to help their children continue to enjoy athletic participation and to reap its many benefits.

What Is Burnout?

What overuse can do to young athletes' cartilage and growth plates, overexposure can do to their interest and enthusiasm. Each damages the child in a different way. Youngsters are more deeply involved in sports than they have ever been. As indicated earlier in this book, some pre-high school and high school kids are playing as many as 100 basketball games in a single season. The reasons for such overexposure are as compelling to kids as they are varied to you and me.

The rewards of success in sports are very alluring. Recent statistics indicate, for example, that as many as 40 percent of inner city black athletes *expect* to play professional basketball. "Expect" is the operative word. The fact that such an expectation is statistically hopeless doesn't stop these kids from wanting it or aiming for it. The few who find it show younger kids that the fame and fortune of professional basketball can be found at the end of that yellow brick road that leads them daily into gymnasiums and playgrounds.

There are other reasons. If professional sports isn't the goal, a college scholarship might be—or a shot at being all-conference or all-state. More obviously, kids just enjoy being with friends, learning how to be better athletes, or sharing in the tradition they have read so much about. Whatever the reasons, kids are discovering that their enjoyment of a certain sport also involves a heightened commitment to winning and to the mastery of the sport's fundamental and advanced skills. At this point, something has to give: the child's school work, his home life—or the sport.

Even children with exceptional talent and dedication run out of gas. Obviously, some kids hang on and move from one level of competition to the next with a growing commitment to be the best they can be. These are the children who often merge their sports with their self-concepts and squeeze out other important aspects of their lives. But most kids, a significant majority, want other things in their lives, too. These are the kids who are finding it harder and harder to keep sports in perspective, given the time and emotional commitment that are demanded by growing numbers of coaches and parents. Parents must be sensitive to this growing problem and know how to deal with it.

Burnout is not fatigue. Athletes, young or old, certainly don't perform or learn as well when fatigued. But being tired doesn't mean that they are burned out. When fatigued athletes revive their oxygen and strength levels, they usually resume acceptable levels of learning and performance.

When oxygen and strength levels are not in question, however, and athletes still fail to learn and perform, burnout may be an actual or potential problem.

Burnout is not the same as a slump. Sometimes an athlete's performance may decline without a perceptible change in execution. What results is a slump, the decreased ability to hit in baseball or shoot free throws in basketball. Often, what is needed to remedy the problem is feedback from an experienced coach. Sometimes, staleness may be the problem, and the athlete may need a break from the routine. The need for such a break may signal the onset of burnout.

Distinguishing among burnout, staleness, or a slump, therefore, is not easy. One may be independent of the other, or one may signal the onset of the other. Fortunately, there are other signs of burnout (we will discuss them in this chapter). In addition, some kids, based upon their personality types, are more disposed to burnout than others. As a parent, you must be familiar with these signals in order to help a child who may be in danger of burning out, quitting a sport, and missing out on what might have been one of the most memorable experiences of his or her life.

Five Personality Traits That Lead to Burnout

Some personality types are more susceptible to burnout than others. If your children possess one or more of these characteristics, watch them closely. They might not experience burnout, but they may be predisposed to it:

Perfectionism. Perfectionists settle for nothing but their absolute best. They set high standards for themselves and struggle mightily to achieve them.

Often many of these standards are unachievable, so, in spite of the several successes they experience, they eventually become frustrated and disappointed.

We had a team one year that was undefeated and unscored on during their first four games of the season. Getting more excited with each successive game, they decided that their goal for the year was to be unscored on. I suggested that they be a little more realistic, but they set the goal in spite of me. Early in our fifth game, the opposing team scored a touchdown, then another and another. We lost the game 32-0—and didn't win another game that year.

Okay, it might have been my fault for not insisting that this team focus on a goal that was more achievable. It's important, however, to recognize that most of us play into the perfectionism of our kids. We admire their drive, their hard work, and their desire to achieve. Research, in fact, indicates that most coaches want these kinds of kids on their teams. But we all have to be careful. Kids who drive themselves relentlessly to achieve their goals may deserve our respect, but they also need our help to achieve a better balance in their lives. Nothing is more shocking to us than the sudden realization that we're not as good as we think we are.

Says sports psychologist, D. A. Feigley: "While dedication to a sport is essential for high-level success, if one's focus is too narrow, too intense, or too prolonged at too early an age, the likelihood of burnout increases dramatically."

Passivity. Passive children tend to accept orders and direction with little regard for their own opinions or feelings. Because it's hard for them to express anger or other emotions without feeling guilty, they tend to internalize their feelings. Internalized and unexpressed anger often turns into depression, and depression results in a loss of energy. This loss of energy is one of the biggest causes of burn out.

High sensitivity to criticism. We are all sensitive to criticism. How we react to it depends on the nature of the criticism. A little constructive criticism is usually okay, especially if the child asks for it. The best time for any kind of evaluation is when people ask for it. But most critics are folks who knock without entering! They share random judgments with little regard for the other's feelings or without ever having faced similar problems.

Smart parents and coaches understand this. When they criticize, they make sure to spread more light than heat. When our criticism illuminates, it improves performance. When it simply spreads heat, it makes kids uncomfortable—some more than others. Uncomfortable kids don't learn, and the most sensitive among them suffer the loss of energy that leads to burnout.

I used to tell each of my athletes early in the year to imagine a can of duck spray in their hands. I told them, "Listen to and learn from your coaches and others in your life, but when people become too negative or hurtful, pull out the can, spray it on yourself, and— like a duck—let the pain of their comments roll off your back. Then get back to work—to being the best you can be."

Impulsivity. Volatile, impulsive kids live on the emotional edge. They tend to react emotionally and sometimes carelessly to people and things in their lives. Their behavior leads most of us to believe that they have an excess of energy, and usually they do. But this supply of energy sometimes runs out. When it does, impulsive kids lose an important emotional resource and can experience minor depression. This depression, no matter how brief, can lead to burnout.

Ego-driven. Show me the child or the teenager who isn't driven by ego. As a coach and, for that matter, as a parent, I accepted this in my kids. Psychologist Erich Fromm said, "Man can be defined as the animal that can say 'I', that can be aware of itself as a separate entity." A child driven by ego has a clear sense of direction. That kids must regard themselves as deserving individuals is critical in their development toward healthy adulthood. But when ego becomes synonymous with self-interest, we run into trouble. Such kids think only of themselves and want everything their way. They usually get burned out and quit when they discover that the world doesn't see eye to eye with them.

Responding to Signs of Burnout

If your child possesses one of these five personality traits, he or she is a candidate for burnout. Be especially alert if he or she reflects one of the following behaviors. They are sure signs of burnout. They might signal other problems as well, but when kids seem reluctant to go to practice or to get excited about contests, these signs warrant your attention:

- Apparent unwillingness to talk

- General anxiety

- Inability to concentrate

- Expressionless

- Irritable

- Constantly tired

When parents observe any of these signals, they should respond immediately to remedy the problem. A failure to respond quickly allows the problem to grow until it may be too late to do anything about it. Here are some effective responses:

More isn't better. The National Collegiate Athletic Association (NCAA) has cut back on the amount of time college athletes can participate in a sport. Even with such restrictions, some coaches still find ways to cheat, to lengthen their seasons to get more practice time. Such coaches are convinced that "more is better," that if two hours of practice teaches fundamental and advanced skills, four hours will teach twice as many.

The NCAA had good reason for cutting back on the length of seasons. Such overexposure leads to a disregard for other aspects of each athlete's life and, ultimately, to burnout. This is especially true for young kids. If your child's coach is requiring too much of your child's time, have a talk with the coach. And don't feel uncomfortable about telling the coach how to do his or her job. That isn't the reason for your conversation. The reason is to discuss the amount of time your child is involved in practice or contests. Some coaches are so focused on the athlete in "student-athlete" that they disregard the rest of the child. Parents can't let that happen.

More games are just as bad. Some young basketball players spend months playing in one league or tournament after another. Just because a child loves basketball doesn't mean that this kind of involvement is good for him or her. Kids love candy and television, too. But a steady diet of both is unhealthy. The same is true of sports. Help your child put such involvement in perspective and find the time to grow in other important areas of his or her life. It sounds corny, but have the child take dinner over to a sick neighbor or relative or cookies to an elderly neighbor. Just being good is always better than being good at something.

Help them avoid too much stress. Have you ever noticed in a basketball game how the rim actually seems to shrink for the team that's under stress because they're losing? It doesn't matter how good the team is either. Even potential national champions don't play well under stress. Okay, we're all under stress; it's becoming a way of life. But it's an observable fact that athletes who are pressured to win are under more stress than other athletes and burn out much faster.

My daughter shared this story about a teammate of my grandson's. The boy's mother yells almost constantly at her son. When she yells, the boy plays worse and worse. Yesterday, she wasn't at the game, and the boy scored more points, got more rebounds, and cooperated more with his teammates than ever before.

Pushing them makes matters worse. The harder we push, the worse kids do, probably because they feel even more stress. To compete successfully and to avoid burnout, kids need frequent expressions of confidence and support. They need to feel good about themselves and to be assured that they *can* improve their performance. Without such assurances, most kids try too hard, and they forget many of the advanced skills they learned previously.

Keep this principle in mind: When kids are under stress, they regress to previously learned behaviors. Many coaches and parents are unfamiliar with this principle. Smart coaches and parents understand it and help kids learn how to handle stress rather than create more of it for them. In other words, it's easier for kids to perform as expected and avoid burnout when stress is manageable. Stress is *not* manageable for them when coaches or parents push them too hard, yell at them, or allow them to create unreasonable or extreme goals for themselves.

Give them choices to make. Kids make primary, not secondary, commitments to a sport and are less inclined to burn out when they are encouraged to make decisions about the sport. First and foremost, the child should make the decision to participate in the sport. Youngsters who are pushed into a particular sport are usually unable to make a total commitment to it. At that point, the decision to participate is someone else's, and any obstacles they encounter along the way are reasons to burn out.

In addition, parents and coaches who ask kids about their opinions regarding strategy and technique create commitment in them. Good coaches understand that when a number of kids help the team decide how to prepare for an upcoming opponent, they will do everything they can to make the plan successful. Parents can help as well by discussing similar decisions over the dinner table. The child's decisions to work hard that week, to focus on performance, and to learn assignments help create commitment and prevent burnout.

Help with tension after competition. Sometimes, the emotions an athlete experiences *after* competition are the toughest to handle. Depression is probably the most difficult because it can attack kids for some of the strangest reasons. Take the biggest victory of the season. Preparation for the contest and the contest itself can push kids into such emotional highs that when the contest is over, they have nowhere to go but down.

We beat one of the best teams in the state one year en route to a state championship. On the way home in a car full of coaches, I found myself feeling absolutely terrible. I recall asking my colleagues what the heck was going on with me. One of them said, "You're crashing. Happens all the time to me after a big game."

One of the real pleasures of athletic participation is the excitement of playing outstanding opponents. It involves a pulse-pounding, sustained challenge that forces athletes to reach new levels of commitment and performance. Because it is so emotionally charged and can't be sustained indefinitely, it also involves "crashing," the unavoidable down period that follows. Such a down period can lead to burnout.

Depression also affects the several kids on the team who may not have played in the contest. Their frustration and disappointment can lead to levels of depression that make them question their continuing participation. "Why do I keep doing this just to get my head beat in in practice?" "I'm as good as she is and I never get to play." "Maybe this sport just isn't for me. I think I'm wasting my time." When kids start making such comments, burnout is unavoidable.

Four Things Parents Can Do to Relieve Tension After a Contest

To combat the effects of "crashing" or the depression that results from not playing, parents must:

1. Provide emotional support after each contest, whether the child wins or loses. Such support involves encouraging the child to express his or her feelings, to empathize with those feelings, to help clarify his or her thinking, and just to be with him or her as much as possible.

2. Spend time with your child after the game. Suggest some kind of family activity: going out to dinner, taking in a movie, or just having a nice, relaxing evening at home. The child may want to be with his or her friends after the big game, but sometimes this is the *worst* time for kids to get together. Their depression or continuing euphoria often results in drinking, fighting, or other extreme behaviors.

3. Help your child reflect on his or her performance, and refrain from imposing your own judgments. Kids have to learn how to self-evaluate and self-criticize. The period of time after a contest is one of the best times to teach both. Also help the child who didn't play by focusing on plans for the future: to work harder on fundamental skills, to learn more about the sport in anticipation of next year's involvement, or to recognize the important contributions he or she makes during practice.

The arms and legs of a team are the kids who play in the contests. The heart of any team is the many kids who selflessly commit themselves to playing against the starters in practice and to cheering for them in contests. They may not play much in contests, but they have genuine courage. They are indispensable elements of any team because they often become inspirations to the other players on the team.

4. Orient your child to the future. This contest may have involved a crashing victory or a crushing defeat and, as such, warrants the self-reflection that your child can learn from it. But never forget that the game is over— and life goes on. There's another contest next week or a big homework assignment tomorrow. Get the child's mind back on his or her responsibilities, and burnout is unlikely.

Emphasize the need to have fun. All of us, kids included, continue to do things that are enjoyable. If it hurts, we don't want to do it. It's that simple. So teach your child to adjust to the coach who yells too much, or take the time to talk to the coach yourself. Do it discreetly, but share your concerns about your child's growing unwillingness to stay on the team. Youth activities and secondary school programs are too important to kids to allow lousy coaches to destroy the simple joy of participation and to cause countless kids to burn out and quit.

Five Ways to Deal With Burnout in the Young Athlete

If your child is already burned out and is talking about quitting, fortunately you can still help. Admittedly, the going is a lot tougher, but quick intervention can help the child reconsider his or her options. Use one or more of the following strategies when helping your child:

1. *Recognize that enough is enough.* If the child is tired and run down, burnout may seem to be the immediate problem, and it might be. More likely, however, the child simply needs some time away from the sport. Discuss this possibility with the child and his or her coach. Don't pull her out of the next big game when her team may be counting on her, but consider skipping that tournament that starts as soon as the current season is over.

2. *Help the child deal with anger.* Being outplayed, making mistakes, failing to learn an assignment or master a skill, being criticized unfairly or excessively, or being slighted in other ways all lead to frustration, which leads to anger. Such anger can be externalized in the form of aggression or internalized in the form of depression. Both are bad. Unchecked aggression can lead to a loss of self-control, and depression can lead to mistakes, poor performance, and the decision to quit. The point is, when parents reduce or eliminate the anger, the child's decision is likely to change.

Here are four ways to help kids deal with anger:

- Reason defeats anger. Take the time to reason with the child. A logical and reasonable approach with children can make even the worst situation more acceptable.

- Use reason even in contrived situations. At appropriate times, ask your child: "What will you do if your coach hurts your feelings?" "What if you miss your first five shots?" "How will you feel about your sport if you get lots of aches and pains or are really tired?" Reflecting about such issues beforehand defuses anger or burnout if and when the issues really happen.

- Help kids distinguish between aggressive and assertive behavior. Children who learn positive ways to assert themselves when they're angry don't internalize their anger. The anger rarely causes depression. They learn also that aggression usually makes a situation worse and that assertiveness usually solves it. Learning to stand up for themselves helps kids develop a positive self-concept and avoid burnout.

- Model appropriate behavior. Expect coaches to model it, too. The coach who rants and raves up and down the sideline throwing bottles of Gatorade may think of himself as charismatic, but he's a loser. The parent who sits in the stands screaming at her child may be satisfying some peculiar need in herself, but she's only hurting her child and making a spectacle of herself. Parents and coaches want to be leaders, and we can't lead if we're standing in the back of the pack kicking our kids in the rear end. It's hard to lead resentful kids. They don't want to follow.

3. *Promote a positive outlook.* All young athletes, all kids for that matter, must learn the power of positive

self-talk. The child who struggles with free throws will continue to struggle with them if she thinks only about her last ten misses. "I just can't make a free throw. That's all there is to it. I just can't feel the shot." Such thinking causes the child to focus on all her bad habits, and one thing is for sure. She *won't* feel the shot, and she *will* miss it.

She has to learn how to create positive images, to think about and—in her mind—to "see" herself successfully shoot free throws. "Keep your eye on the basket; don't aim the shot, feel it roll off your fingers, and make a good follow through." This kind of focus results in successful free throw attempts. Similarly, the child walking into a big test has to see himself getting a good score, believing that he will do well. If he thinks only of failure, that's what he's likely to do.

Children who think positive thoughts believe in themselves. Such kids are success-oriented. My young running back in the story at the end of chapter four genuinely believed that he wouldn't be tackled during the scrimmage. He was tackled—many times—but he continued to believe in himself, to "see" himself running sixty yards for a touchdown. Finally, he did. Success is only a short distance away when kids persist in believing in themselves.

When kids don't think positively, burnout is just around the corner. So if your child is burned out and talks about quitting, make a quick assessment of his or her state of mind. If the child is full of negative thoughts, now's the time for you to share one of life's valuable lessons: "You can do anything you want in life, if you want it badly enough and if you're willing to pay the price." Such a lesson causes kids to recommit to important goals. It's also important to recognize that kids can't pay the price unless they believe in themselves, whether they're playing soccer, studying equations, or deciding to join the chess club. And they believe in themselves when we believe in them. Such belief creates positive thinking and transforms "I quit," into "Let's give it one more try."

4. *Help the child reconsider his or her goals.* Most kids play sports to be with friends and to have some fun. They burn out and decide to quit when they lose sight of these goals. The child who is burned out simply isn't having fun. It's that simple. You as a parent can do four things:

- Help the child redefine "fun." Sports involve highly disciplined activities. That's one of the reasons why we want our kids to be involved. For some kids, the self-discipline and hard work involved in making a maximum effort are not "fun." The child who discovers that "fun" involves a sense of accomplishment and self-satisfaction learns an important lesson in life and is likely to recommit to athletic competition.

- Help the child refocus on positive performance. I learned early in my playing career, maybe as early as elementary school, that my attitude and enthusiasm changed every time I tried to change the attitudes and enthusiasm of my teammates. This could be good as well as bad. My lousy attitude had a bad effect, and my positive attitude had a good one. I got fired up every time I tried to fire them up. If your child refocuses on friends, he or she may recommit to the sport.

- Consider the development of short-term rather than long-term goals. A losing season is discouraging to even the most dedicated athlete. When the outcome of the season, even the outcome of a particular contest, is the goal, the immediate joy of participation is lost. Help the child refocus on the satisfaction of gaining new skills or performing old skills well, enjoying friends, or being the kind of kid who is willing to work hard and commit to difficult tasks. Such a renewed focus may change his or her mind about quitting.

- Talk to the coach. When your child has decided to quit a sport, you have every right to talk to the coach. When coaches discover that their players aren't enjoying the experience, most of them do some serious soul-searching. Some actually reintroduce enjoyable activities during practice—after all, 90 percent of athletic participation involves practice. If the coach is incapable of such soul-searching, maybe your child is right to want to quit.

5. *Recognize that quitting may be the only answer.* Sometimes burnout happens quickly, and the child's decision to quit is correct. Some children simply don't have the body types, abilities, or necessary temperament to compete in certain sports. They like the sport from afar, but up close, it just doesn't have the same appeal. If you agree with the child's desire to quit, both of you have to consider some important time factors before making the final decision:

- If the child has been involved in the sport for only a few days, have the child stick it out for another week or so. No one, parent or child, is able to decide about an activity after being involved for only a few days. Negotiate with the child to continue for another week, after which time he or she can reconsider the decision to quit. But if the child still wants to quit, it's his or her decision.

- If the child has been involved in the sport for a few weeks and wants to quit, the degree of his or her involvement is important. Has the child become a factor in the coach's planning? Has the child been selected as one of the top players or, at least, as a regular participant? If so, quitting should not be an option. The team is now counting on the child. The decision now affects more than one person.

- If the child has been involved for a few weeks and is simply warming the bench or standing around in practice, quitting is a very real option. If you as a parent agree with the decision, have the child talk to the coach, explain why he or she wants to quit, and then help the child stick to the decision.

- If the child has been involved for at least half the season or more, quitting probably is not an option. It's the child's decision not to join the team next year, but the child risks being called a quitter if he or she already committed to most of the current season. That may be the child's self-assessment, too.

- During your discussions, you may discover or suspect other reasons for the child's desire to quit. Probe her thinking for these reasons. She probably wants to talk about them anyway. She may be fighting with one or more teammates, losing patience with an abusive coach, being teased by her peer group, or hiding a nagging injury. Obviously, each of these problems is different from burnout and requires a different solution. Once resolved, the child might recommit to her sport.

A Few Final Suggestions

Finally, let's consider a few practical tips, the kind that are easily overlooked.

Make a weekly schedule with your child. Include everything in it and be sure the child helps make it. She'll commit to it if she has input. Schedule everything: school work, practice time, chores around the house, TV time—even time on the phone! Formalize the schedule by making copies each week and posting them conspicuously in the kitchen and the child's room. Then make sure the child follows it. This point is particularly important. If disregarded even a little, the child learns nothing about commitments elsewhere in her life and risks burnout.

Prioritize responsibilities. When making the schedule or just discussing the importance of sports, help the child set priorities. A reasonable and realistic look at the important things in life puts sports somewhere near the bottom of the list—this from a coach of thirty-one years! I'm the first to recognize that the child's identity as "Tom, the football player" must necessarily take a back seat to "Tom, the family member," "Tom, the student," "Tom, the churchgoer," and probably most importantly, "Tom, the good guy." Like you, I understand that our society needs more good guys. I also realize that good guys and good gals win, and because they have a range of interests, they don't burn out from overexposure to one sport.

Keep the lines of communication open. Smart parents understand their biggest role in any kind of communication with their children. *Listen.* Ask good questions and listen to the answers. Then probe the answers or ask the child to elaborate in order to encourage his or her reflective thinking. Kids who learn how to self-reflect make good decisions in their lives, the kinds of decisions that avoid burnout. They learn how to choose among alternatives and to realize and accept the consequence of their decisions. They also learn how easy it is to talk to mom and dad.

Albert Camus once wrote: "Don't walk in front of me; I may not follow. Don't walk behind me; I may not lead. Just walk beside me and be my friend."

Don't push; don't even pull. "I'm my child's parent, not his friend." Baloney. I'm the first to agree that some adults spend too much time being pals rather than parents to their kids. Of course this is wrong. But it's also wrong to think that we can't be both to our children. Sometimes pushing and pulling have to take a back seat to simply walking beside children and being their friends. In fact, this may be the best way to help your kids adjust to the demands of playing a sport and avoiding burnout. Empathize, be understanding, be supportive. Don't push.

You Don't Want to Burn Out Either

Sometimes parents have to be almost as careful as kids not to overextend themselves. In our zeal to be all things to all people, we sometimes feel *ourselves* burning out. This is bad for us *and* for our kids. We begin to feel imposed on and often get a little cranky. To avoid this possibility, think about the following suggestions.

Be sure kids put their stuff away after practice or contests. Some sports involve a whole lot of "stuff." Shoulder pads, helmets, baseball mitts, bats and balls, soccer shoes, football cleats, basketballs, basketball shoes, and assorted dirty uniforms often clutter every corner of the house. Things got so bad upstairs in our house that I thought the only way to get into my daughters' rooms was on horseback.

We finally laid down the law. Make sure you do, too. We put a box by the back door and told the kids to put everything in it. Each item my wife or I had to pick up cost them one dollar of allowance.

A friend told her son that it would cost him a quarter every time she picked up an item of clothing or a piece of equipment. At the end of the first week, she told him that he owed her two dollars and fifty cents. While paying her, the boy said, "Here you go, Mom. Keep up the good work."

That was one reason why we decided on a dollar. Famed college basketball coach, John Wooden, once shared with me his philosophy of discipline: "Make the rules clear and the penalties severe." The dollar may not have been severe, but it sure got their attention.

Organize a car pool. "We're all in this together!" should be the rallying cry of all parents, especially if they find themselves covering more miles than the local cabbie. The parents you call are probably as anxious as you are to unburden themselves of driving to and from practices, meetings, and contests. You might feel safer driving your child to and from games that are far away, but local practices are the big time consumers. Share the magic!

Just say no. Emotionally healthy kids don't learn much from emotionally unhealthy parents. Your frame of mind is critical to the development of your kids. It's also moderately important to you. One of the healthiest things any parent can do, then, is just say no. "I'm sorry, honey, but I'm busy now." "That will have to wait, sweetheart. I have to finish this now." Or the best thing to say? Often better than saying no? "I'm sorry, honey, but what do you plan to do about it?"

That's right, your willingness to just say no does more than anything else to create self-reliant kids. So when Susie complains about a dirty uniform, say "Yes, it is dirty. What do you plan to do about it?" Or Tom may plead, "I forgot I have a practice in five minutes; can you drive me?" Your best response? "Gee, I'm sorry. Tom. What do you plan to do about it?"

Poet William Blake said, "No bird soars too high if it soars with its own wings."

Let's Wrap It Up

Some kids are predisposed to burnout. Youngsters who constantly strive for perfection or who are volatile, passive, or sensitive to criticism warrant careful watching. Kids with these personality traits may need a lot of help from their parents and others.

Other young athletes burn out because of outside factors, such as poor coaching, overexposure to a sport, or undue pressure from friends or family.

Burnout results from other factors as well. One of the most important involves the reasons for the child's involvement in the first place. Most children join sports for the excitement, fun, and opportunity to make new friends or to be with old ones. Some join for the awards, recognition, and social status. Some of these reasons are better than others, but they are all legitimate. All of our needs are different, so are the ways we satisfy them.

As legitimate as these reasons may be, however, they can also create problems. I'm the first to admit that sports are exciting and fun and that they provide recognition, social opportunities, and awards. In fact, athletic participation can provide more sustained excitement than almost anything else a child can do. But the reality remains. Athletic participation is hard work. In addition to its excitement and recognition, it involves occasional pain, overexertion, reasonable but relentless discipline, and personal sacrifice. Children who fail to understand this or who are unable to adjust to the expectations of certain sports soon burn out.

Children who make such adjustments, however, take giant strides toward adulthood. They learn commitment, cooperation, self-control, and the importance of performance over outcome. They experience the rewards of hard work, the need to share success or failure, the value of making a total effort, and the importance of refusing to quit in the pursuit of worthwhile goals. Children who learn such lessons find self-satisfying experiences in sports, and when they do—they don't burn out.

6.
THE REAL WORLD OF ATHLETIC SCHOLARSHIPS

Did You Know?

- High school athletes who receive questionnaires from universities are still facing odds of *320:1* of getting a scholarship.

- Even if a university provides an all-expenses paid trip to the school and wines and dines the recruit and his or her parents, the odds are still 3:1 *against* a scholarship offer.

- In the average high school, only one senior football player—*in every five years*—can expect to receive a scholarship to a major university.

- Among both boys and girls in the average high school, only one senior basketball player in every *ten* to *fifteen* years can expect to receive a scholarship to a major university.

- Of all high school seniors playing football, only one out of 12,500 ever plays in the pros.

Many of us think that motivation is what we do to someone else. That's true, but not completely. Coaches and parents motivate in lots of ways, when they give pep talks, criticize mistakes, or even praise effort. Textbooks call that *external* motivation. They also indicate that even when it involves praise, it's the least effective kind of motivation.

The most effective kind of motivation is when coaches create the environment that enables athletes to satisfy their own needs. That's called *internal* motivation. Internal motivation operates in all of us, and it is the most powerful kind of motivation because we always have needs that must be satisfied. We have a variety of them, and most of our behavior results from our attempts to satisfy them.

Our needs motivate all our behaviors. Socially, we need to belong, to relate to and to be accepted by others. That's why being on a team is so important to many kids. Playing the sport may be fun, but equally important is the need to belong to a group with which they identify strongly. The social need to belong is a powerful motivator and, if unsatisfied, it can be profoundly disappointing. Being accepted is one of our most compelling social needs.

As quoted in the **Notre Dame Magazine,** *Michael Jordan once said, "For about two weeks, every boy who had tried out for the basketball team knew the day the cut list was going to be up. So that morning we all went in there, and the list was up. We stood there and looked for our names. If your name was on the list, you were still on the team. If your name wasn't on the list, you were cut. Mine wasn't on the list. I looked and looked for my name. But I wasn't there. I went through the day numb. I sat through my classes. I had to wait until after school to go home. That's when I hurried to my house and closed the door to my room and I cried so hard. It was all I wanted—to play on that team."*

Interestingly, being accepted is also one of our most important ego needs. That's the focus of this chapter. Once a child "makes the team" and discovers and demonstrates athletic ability, the recognition he or she receives satisfies a very important ego need. We all need recognition and a sense of accomplishment. Participation in athletics provides many of our most satisfying and memorable accomplishments. Invariably, they motivate us to try for more.

The good news and the bad news. That involves some good news and some bad news. The good news is that sports teaches youngsters lasting lessons about the importance of hard work and commitment, and it does more for their self-confidence than most people realize. It also opens the door to continued recognition in the form of honors, even scholarships to continue playing their sports in college.

That's where the bad news comes in. The bad news is that many youngsters, even many parents, fail to realize just how difficult it is to earn an athletic scholarship. Some families are convinced that if junior earns all-conference honors by being the top scorer on his high school basketball team, he deserves a scholarship to play for Duke or Kansas. Wanting the best for our kids means we love them, but we can't let our love blind us to some important realities.

Young athletes deserve everything that sports can give them, especially the few who work harder than everyone else on the team and seem to have genuine talent. A reality of athletic competition in this country, however, is the farther one goes in a sport, the greater the rewards may be—but the harder they are to get. Earning all-star, even all-state honors is one thing. Receiving an athletic scholarship to a major university to play against the finest football, basketball, tennis, or volleyball players in the world is another.

Size and speed alone don't favor most kids. Rarities just a few years ago, three-hundred-pound linemen in football and 6'7" women in basketball are virtually commonplace today. What's more, they are stronger and faster than their smaller counterparts of only a few years ago. It's not uncommon for linemen today to bench press 500 pounds or for backs to run 4.3 forties. Even more amazing is that some of these backs weigh as much as 225 pounds.

I was a 235-pound fullback when I played at Nebraska. I remember my first scrimmage. My assignment was to block one of our defensive tackles, the biggest player I had ever seen—6'6" and 320 pounds. I remember thinking, "Well, here's my chance. I'm gonna really hit this guy to let everyone know that I've arrived!" I know one thing. If he's reading this book , this is probably the first time he discovered that I hit him.

Most linemen in college *average* that much today. They're as big as most pro players. Seven-footers in basketball and 6'4" women in volleyball are just as commonplace. Unfortunately, many parents and kids fail to realize this.

As reported in the Chicago Sun-Times just a few years ago, "Parents must realize that there are hundreds of kids who have great hearts, made all-state teams, and have been very productive in high school. . . . But colleges don't see any of that. All they ask is, 'Does he/she project to being a great player in college?'"

So let's be realistic. Most of us hate anyone to tell us to "be realistic." It's a saying that always signals bad news. And the bad news is that most recruiters base such projections on size and speed. Yes, I know, they overlook lots of kids who are smaller and a bit slower but who could become great college players. Unfortunately, their bigger and faster counterparts are in for all the attention from college recruiters. That's just the way it is.

Fortunately, there is still much we can do to get the attention of college scouts. The first thing parents and kids must do, however, is realistically assess appropriate levels of competition. Is this boy or girl *realistically* a Division I prospect? Should he or she consider Division II or Division III programs? Talk to coaches and former players to make such decisions. Then do everything outlined in this chapter to get the attention of scouts and to assure that the youngster is qualified both academically and athletically to play at that level.

Above all, recognize that the love of our children usually requires us to take a step or two backward to do what is right for them. The worst thing we can do is allow their successes to become *our* successes. Some of us are so intent on getting the best for our kids or identifying so strongly with their accomplishments that we overestimate their athletic ability. Invariably, this leads to frustration, anger, and disappointment for everyone when the scholarship grows further and further out of reach. One of our jobs as parents is to help our kids understand that if they continually dream of the person they would like to be—they will waste the person they are.

Sometimes it leads to pain. We had a wide receiver one year who had the uncanny ability to find open spots in the opponent's defense. He was only 5'10" and 180 pounds, and he ran only a 5.2 forty. If you're unfamiliar with the speed of wide receivers, that's pretty slow, but he did manage to set several school records because of his good hands and ability to get open. He was so good in high school that his dad wanted him to play for Michigan.

There was no way he could play for Michigan and, in spite of our repeated warnings, his dad talked to a friend at Michigan who allowed the boy to "walk on," in essence to be on Michigan's team without a scholarship. Playing for the "hamburgers" (that's the team of fifth and sixth stringers who scrimmage against the first team) in his *first* scrimmage, he caught a pass over the middle and got hit by a 260-pound middle linebacker. His brief tenure at Michigan ended that day.

Kids who perform these roles on any team are dedicated, great kids. But coaches have to watch them carefully to avoid mismatches. Parents have to be careful, too. Be as realistic as possible about your child's chances to play for a college program. Just one mismatch on the college level can result in lifelong disability.

What Is an Athletic Scholarship?

A scholarship is a lot of things. It represents an expense-free trip to college, a preliminary assessment of athletic ability, and, unfortunately, a sometimes very misleading look at the future. It is the goal of thousands of young athletes every year because it's an affirmation of their athletic ability and a big step toward a professional career. Even if professional sports seems unrealistic, it's a clear indication that "someone wants you"—an ego booster that culminates years of hard work in high school.

By definition, an athletic grant-in-aid is a form of financial aid from a college that pays tuition and fees, room and board, and books. It is guaranteed for only one year at a time, although some schools provide a verbal (never written) guarantee for up to five years. Other schools, particularly those rebuilding sagging programs, take scholarships back after one or two years if, in the estimation of the coaches, the athlete fails to perform up to par or gets injured.

This uncertainty of a scholarship and of any athlete's continuing opportunity to play a sport in college requires kids and their families to focus on academics. Sports for most kids is a secondary reason for going to college. I'm the first to admit that an athletic scholarship is a boon to family finances. I received one to play football in college; my youngest daughter received one to play basketball. I learned that it helps immeasurably with the "dollars" aspect of a college education. The "sense" aspect, however, is up to the family—and the National Collegiate Athletic Association (NCAA).

Let's look first at the requirements of the NCAA. Not many years ago, the admissions offices of many colleges and universities rivaled their fine arts departments for unbridled creativity. They had a variety of ways to evaluate high school transcripts, especially of promising athletes. To say that some kids with lousy academic backgrounds received scholarships to play in college is probably one of the great understatements of this book. Many of these kids—if the school could keep them eligible— inspired everyone with their athletic genius but were less than inspirational in the classroom.

So, in 1983 at their convention in San Diego, the NCAA debated what was to become Proposition 48, now bylaw 14.3. Bylaw 14.3 requires all student athletes to meet minimal standards in order to qualify for a scholarship. These standards are subject to change, so the following is only a general overview of NCAA requirements. For specific and updated information, call your high school counselor or athletic director or write the NCAA for a copy of their *Guide for the College-Bound Student-Athlete.*

Generally, to be considered a "qualifier" and to receive a scholarship to a Division I college or university, all student-athletes must:

- Graduate from high school,

- Complete a Core Curriculum of at least thirteen academic units:

  - four in English,

  - two in math,

  - two in science (see your child's counselor for the specifics of these requirements),

  - one more in either English, math, or science,

  - two in social studies,

  - two additional.

- Satisfy the grade point average requirements in these courses while earning an appropriate score on the ACT (American College Testing program) or the SAT (Scholastic Aptitude Test). This requirement involves a sliding scale that allows the student athlete to compensate for a lower grade point average with higher test scores and vice versa. Again, contact your child's coach, counselor, or the appropriate NCAA bulletin for specific information.

The NCAA has also established additional standards for young athletes who fall short of these requirements. Such athletes are called "partial qualifiers" and must satisfy the requirements of a different sliding scale. Again, talk to high school personnel to familiarize yourself with these requirements. Failure to satisfy all of them means that your child is a "nonqualifier" and will have to either postpone or abandon any idea of receiving a scholarship to play in a major college.

Every athlete in our school learned quickly that the day of the "dumb athlete" is over. Put yourself in the size fourteens of a young linemen who is expected to know how to block a "Crossfire tackle trap at five" versus a "wide tackle six," a "fifty-two tackles inside," or a "gap stack forty-four." Understanding how to do this involves a thought process that rivals the toughest math class.

Bylaw 14.3, when it was still Proposition 48, provoked a whole lot of controversy. The good news is that it halted the influx of unqualified students into our nation's universities and reaffirmed the fundamental purpose of higher education. The bad news is that it introduced a range of very specific course, grade point, and test score requirements that befuddled thousands of counselors, coaches, and athletic directors across the country.

Such confusion is still evident in many schools. Every year, stories of misinformed youngsters fill sports pages everywhere. Invariably, each of these young athletes—and their parents—have to jump through one bureaucratic hoop after another to rectify the problem. Sometimes the problems aren't rectified and the youngster has to sit out a year or more of competition.

This means that parents must be more involved than ever in helping their children select courses, maintain records, and sign up at appropriate times for SAT and ACT tests. Rare is the school counselor who can keep track of his or her high school's curriculum, the periodic misbehavior of hundreds of students, changing college entrance requirements, reams of paperwork, *and* the evolving expectations of the NCAA's bylaw 14.3. A lot of the work, therefore, falls to you. Again, it's a good idea to get your own copy of the NCAA's *Guide for the College-Bound Student-Athlete* and to refer to it every time your child registers for high school courses.

Considering the Availability of Athletic Scholarships

This is an important section for families who are considering the possibility of a scholarship. Some of the information may be disappointing, but it provides a realistic look at the very select world of athletic scholarships.

Most high schools are fortunate if just one of their seniors—in every 4 or 5 years—receives a scholarship to play major college football. Parents who watch their child run back a kickoff against their toughest opponent deserve the vision of watching him punch one across in the Rose Bowl, but such expectations are sometimes unrealistic. A "free ride" to play in college may be a bit more realistic than playing in the pros, but scholarships are much less available than most athletes and their parents realize.

How many high school football players and parents realize that major universities mail as many as 5,000 to 8,000 questionnaires each year to prospective high school football players? Of the several thousand high school football players who receive questionnaires from a particular school, therefore, only one in every 320 will receive a scholarship. Even if a high school athlete and his or her parents are given an all-expenses paid visit to a university to be housed, wined, and dined for a weekend, the odds are still 3 to 1 *against* the possibility of a scholarship.

The NCAA allows Division I colleges and universities seventy all-expenses paid visits for prospective football players and their parents. But these schools can award only twenty-five freshman scholarships in football. Because there are only 107 (this number changes periodically but not significantly) Division I schools with football programs, the total number of scholarships awarded annually—nationwide—is roughly 2,675. The NCAA indicates that approximately 275,000 high school seniors play football each year. Only *one percent* of them can hope for a football scholarship to a major university.

My job as a coach has never been to stick pins in balloons. I always encouraged my athletes to cling to their dreams and to work hard to realize them. If a scholarship is your child's goal, help him or her "go for it." Kids need goals. Goals are motivating, and they develop self-discipline. Help your child see that the glass is half full, not half empty, but to see the glass clearly, make sure your child has his or her eyes wide open.

Considering the periodic tidal wave of media coverage about basketball scholarships, the person on the street is likely to believe that countless thousands of high school kids are hounded by college recruiters. Think about the fact that there are just under 300 major college and university basketball programs in this country and that the NCAA allows only thirteen total scholarships per program.

The total number of basketball players attending major colleges through basketball scholarships, therefore, is just under 4,000. Because the majority of them are upperclassmen, it follows that only two or three scholarships per major program are available to incoming freshmen, an approximate total of 900 scholarships available nationwide! Approximately 160,000 high school seniors play basketball each year; only one in every 177 can expect to play for a major college or university, just one half of one percent.

The numbers are similar with women's programs. The NCAA permits more basketball scholarships for women than for men, but the total number of scholarships available for high school senior girls is still just under 1,000, hardly the widespread availability suggested by the media. Like the boys in their schools, therefore, the girls should enjoy the excitement of competitive sports and reap the several benefits of hard work and team commitment, but they had better put the whole scholarship picture in perspective. The primary, sometimes the *exclusive*, reward of athletic competition is excitement and satisfaction, not the future promise of a "free ride."

> *A friend of mine, a coach with thirty-two years experience, used to tell his players, "Nothing is 'free' about a free ride. Between meetings, practices, travel, contests, and training room time, you will 'play the price' of that free ride many times over!"*

Prompted by organizations like the Knight Commission, the NCAA has recently reduced the total number of scholarships in all intercollegiate sports. Men's tennis, for example, now permits only four to five scholarships for the entire team. The same is true of men's volleyball and golf. This means that, during any given year, many schools may have no scholarships available for incoming freshmen. Even in sports like soccer that award eleven team scholarships, the limited number available for freshmen suggests that high school soccer players are competing for only two to three hundred scholarships nationwide.

That parents and school personnel understand these realities is critical if young athletes are to receive the help they need to develop realistic visions of their educational futures. Receiving a scholarship to continue playing a sport in college may be a reasonable goal for many young athletes, but it must never be an expectation. Such an expectation sets kids up for too much disappointment. Maybe more important, kids also begin to see sports as a means to an end and miss out on the immediate pleasures of athletic participation.

Girls and women have made a lot of progress. In 1990, the average athletic department had 332 male athletes and only 130 female athletes. Five years later, because of Title IX, the numbers had changed to 292 men and 163 women in all Division I-A schools. Such progress is likely to continue if those of us who want athletic participation to benefit *everyone* are sensitive to changing opinions and trends.

Girls who play sports are 92 percent less likely to use drugs, 80 percent less likely to get pregnant while still in school, and three times more likely to graduate from high school.

Significant personal gains have been made by girls. In fact, the benefits of athletic participation for girls seem more pronounced than for boys. Whereas drinking seems to increase as boys play multiple sports, the reverse seems to be true of girls. That they continue to have access to sports programs is essential if girls are to receive the help they need to overcome widespread temptations with drugs and recreational sex.

Who Receives Athletic Scholarships?

The obvious answer is that good athletes who are also good students receive athletic scholarships. College recruiters want the best athletes they can find, but even a potential All-American is no good to them if he or she can't compete in the classroom. Beyond that, sports strategy is now so sophisticated that most poor students are unable to learn it. What good is the great jumper or great runner if she runs in the wrong direction?

A close friend of mine at a major university told me once that he will never again recruit a youngster who had trouble meeting the requirements of bylaw 14.3, "These kids just have too much trouble competing on the field and in the classroom. It's not worth it to them or to us."

Another good friend who coaches in college once said to me, "Give me the less talented kid who learns quickly and who is likely to stick around for four years. We'll have time to make a great player out of her."

It stands to reason. The great runner or the great jumper who is also a great student projects to be a great player. Strong, fast, and *smart* make an unbeatable combination. Of all the "blue chippers" out there, the kids with this combination are the most in demand. And, parents, if your child is a blue chipper, get ready for a whole lot of attention.

What is a blue chipper? A blue chipper is a uniquely gifted athlete who is highly recruited by colleges and universities across the country. Blue chippers possess a talent that usually can't be taught.

These are uncoachable talents. Either kids have these kinds of kinesthetic gifts or they don't. If they don't, we can still teach skills to young athletes, and, if they have the desire and work ethic, help them develop into blue chippers. Usually, however, blue chippers are rarities, gifted kids who can't explain their own talents. They simply have them and, usually, they leave the rest of us slack-jawed when we observe them.

> *I worked with a young running back once who was so talented that I actually had other coaches ask me what I was doing to teach him such remarkable skills. I always said the same thing: "Do you want to know the single most important thing I've ever said to him?" The coaches always pleaded, "Yes, yes!" I said, "It's simple. I just stand on the sidelines and shout, 'Run, Billy, run!'"*

And We Want the Best for Them

I developed a fondness early in my career for the youngster with twice the heart and half the talent of his or her more gifted teammates. I watched many of them develop into outstanding high school athletes, and I knew that most of them wanted a college scholarship. I wanted one for them, too. In fact, I wanted the best of everything for them, just as their parents did.

I also knew, however, that kids who aren't big enough or fast enough probably won't get the chance to play in college. Fortunately, I also knew that their hard work and commitment would be rewarded. I've seen too many gritty kids develop into doctors, teachers, lawyers, successful business people, and marvelous parents. Their continuing successes have reaffirmed in my mind that hard work really is its own reward. Parents must not lose sight of this fact.

I know that maintaining such perspective isn't always easy, particularly when you and I see so many gifted kids cruise along on little more than their own talent. But that's true everywhere, from gifted programs in first grade to advanced placement courses in high school. Things come easily to most gifted kids, including the attention they receive.

The NCAA News reported recently that approximately 20,000 street agents, folks who give kids money to help them find college and professional teams, are giving 75 percent of underclassmen illegal cash or gifts. Said the Chicago Sun-Times's Taylor Bell: "[These] rodents in pin-stripe suits and Gucci shoes could create a major scandal in college that will make the Teapot Dome scandal look like a leaky oil filter."

What a lot of us don't realize is that even most high school blue chippers don't play in college. They may dominate the numbers mentioned earlier in this chapter and receive the scholarships, but most soon learn that the world of college athletics is populated by extraordinarily gifted young men and women. I was the fastest player on our high school football team. I led the team in scoring, yards gained, and average yards per carry, but, when I got to college, I sure ate a lot of the dust of all those players who routinely flew past me during wind sprints after practice.

So, what about the youngsters who plan to play in the pros? Well, they're in for a big surprise. A recent study indicates that up to 40 percent of inner-city black kids *expect* to play a professional sport. This statistic wouldn't be so shocking if these kids *hoped* to play professionally. But *expecting* to follow the yellow brick road to the Emerald City's promise of fame and fortune is at best disappointing, at worst tragic.

Approximately 160,000 high school seniors play basketball. Fewer than 100 rookies each year earn spots on a professional team. To put that in perspective, look at the number this way. If your high school had started its basketball program when Abraham Lincoln became president during the Civil War, you'd still have to wait almost 20 *years* for your school's first athlete to play professionally. The odds of playing professional football are a little better, but the fact remains. Most kids, no matter what their socioeconomic circumstances, are far more likely to be hit by lightning or, better, to become doctors and lawyers, than to be professional athletes.

Several years ago, a prominent university sports official indicated that as many as one half of all professional athletes end their careers with no money, a significant percentage of them are divorced, and the life expectancy of many is around sixty.

In disadvantaged areas, however, the word "professional" relates to Michael Jordan and Brett Favre more than to Colin Powell or Johnny Cochran, and, considering the cultural obstacles inner city kids have to battle, a million dollar contract with the New York Knicks seems a whole lot more accessible than Harvard's graduate school. It's no startling revelation to say, therefore, that culture is the problem in the inner city, not just because of the obstacles it creates for kids, but because of the solutions it embraces, especially solutions that are so potentially disappointing to everybody.

The inner city youth who works to become a future president of the United States develops a range of useful and marketable skills even if he or she falls short of that goal. The same child who works to become only an NBA superstar and falls short of that goal is left with skills that have absolutely no value off the basketball court!

Sports and the Classroom

Learning how to slam dunk in high school, therefore, may be fun, but it's occupationally limiting! Rhetoric and quadratic equations may be less exciting than buzzer beaters, but their benefits last a whole lot longer. Enjoying sports, therefore, is a lot of family fun and one of the best ways for parents to connect with their kids, but sports must *never* be allowed to interfere in any way with school work. Sports may teach analytic and reasoning skills and the importance of character in everything we do, but not even the most vigorous athletic program can replace the classroom for important life skills.

So if a sport in college is likely or desirable, young athletes and their parents must follow several important steps. These steps satisfy the requirements of the NCAA but, more importantly, assure that the student is attending a particular college for the right reasons. Use this information as a checklist, therefore, to guarantee that you and your child are addressing all the essential details of selecting a school.

1. *See your counselor.* Meet routinely with your school counselor to be sure your young athlete is in compliance with the requirements of the NCAA's bylaw 14.3. Any failure to satisfy all the requirements of the NCAA will result in his or her inability to play in college. Stories fill the sports pages every year about kids, their counselors, or their parents who simply overlooked one or more requirements and found themselves battling the NCAA bureaucracy. Check and double-check all educational records: registration planning materials, transcripts, four-year plans, anything that documents completion of NCAA requirements.

A college basketball coach, when told that one of his athletes was receiving one D and four F's, said to the youngster, "Son, looks to me like you're spending too much time on one subject."

---

2. *Do a career search.* Most high schools provide comprehensive processes that enable students to explore and choose—at least tentatively—future career goals. They explore personal strengths and weaknesses, personality characteristics, interests, and other variables that relate to career choice. Some searches are so good that many kids actually enter these career areas after graduation from high school or college.

3. *Do a college search.* After choosing at least a tentative career area, explore the colleges and universities that provide academic programs in that area. Obviously, the better the school and the more widely respected the educational program, the more desirable the school will be to you and your child.

4. *Take the ACT and/or the SAT.* Remember that the NCAA has developed a sliding scale that compares the student's grade point average to his or her ACT and/or SAT scores. Again, meet with your counselor or college consultant to make sure your child meets these sliding scale requirements. In fact, refer often to the NCAA pamphlet, *Guide for the College-Bound Student-Athlete,* to make sure he or she is meeting all the requirements of the NCAA.

Six Important Things to Do If You Want a Scholarship

In addition to these four general steps, young athletes and their parents must do several other specific things to increase their chances of getting a scholarship. Be sure to refer often to these six important considerations:

1. *Follow the right process.* Get all the right people involved: your coach, your counselor, your college consultant if your school has one, even your school's athletic director, if appropriate. Maintain ongoing contact with all these people and try to get them all in the same room periodically. Their knowledge of the scholarship and college selection processes will be mutually complementary. What one of them doesn't know, the other will, and you and your child will reap all the benefits.

> *A friend of mine defined intelligent people as "individuals who know what to do—when they don't know what to do." What a great definition. In other words, if you don't know what to do about the scholarship and college search processes, organize a group of people who do. They will provide the answers you need.*

2. *Stay in close contact with your coach.* Check with the coach periodically to see if he or she is:

- maintaining statistics of athletic performance,

- notifying appropriate colleges of the child's talents,

- assuring appropriate press coverage,

- emphasizing the importance of academics,

- informing you and your child of current or changing NCAA requirements.

3. *Develop a resumé.* College recruiters appreciate specific information about scholarship candidates. When the time comes to share a resumé with recruiters, be sure to include the following information: name, address, phone number, date of birth, name of high school, name of school coach, coach's home phone, name of guidance counselor, counselor's school phone, school fax number, the young athlete's academic interests in college, all honors and awards, work experience, athletic statistics/performances, grade point average, class rank, ACT/SAT scores, height, weight, and name of conference.

4. *Develop highlight tapes.* Highlight tapes can be very helpful during the recruiting process—if they are handled correctly. Two kinds of tapes are

generally most helpful. The first shows the young athlete competing in contests, usually against his or her toughest opponents. Get help from commercial technicians or your school's audio-visual department to extract only relevant highlights. Recruiters don't want to watch the entire game. Be sure to include with the tape a stat sheet that specifies the athlete's position and jersey number and identifies the opposing team and its current win-loss record.

The second type of highlight tape is a skill tape. Skill tapes are especially important for sports like track and field, punting and place kicking, field hockey, gymnastics, ice hockey—any sport that involves special, easily observable skills. Sometimes a good skill tape is more helpful to recruiters than game tapes, especially if they are well-produced. Be sure to get help from your child's coach in order to identify all the skills that must be demonstrated.

5. *Learn how to deal with recruiters.* Newspapers and other media outlets have devoted lots of space during recent years to the significant number of student-athletes in colleges and universities who are being "abused" by coaches. My experience has been that the number is not as high as the media would have us believe, but that such abuse is a problem.

Many athletes are sacrificing far too much time to their sports, some to an all-consuming desire to win, many to programs that disregard young athletes' academic and career responsibilities. Thanks to the NCAA, such abuses aren't as prevalent as they were a few years ago, but they still persist on some campuses. I would suggest, however, that for every "abused" student-athlete in college, there are one or more parents, a high school coach, and probably a high school counselor who didn't do his or her job.

The first job of parents, therefore, is to thoroughly evaluate the reputations of college coaches who will be working with your son or daughter for the next four or five years. If that reputation focuses exclusively on winning and/or disregards the importance of academics, look elsewhere. Sports, as important as they seem at the moment, are short-lived in the lives of our kids. A solid education lasts forever. Be sure your child finds it.

Be especially careful of recruiters who use any one of these tactics:

- *Deprecates other programs.* The recruiter who "bum raps" other schools is probably trying to drag them down to his school's level.

- *Praises his own winning program.* If such praise emphasizes the school's win-loss record, it's not good. If it also emphasizes the quality of the school's educational program, it *is* good.

- *Promises an immediate starting position.* The young athlete is indeed rare who can start during his or her first year at a major university.

- *Promises a five-year scholarship.* If such a promise is made, make sure that your child's coach and as many other people as possible also hear it.

- *Involves one or more of their school's "boosters" in recruiting you.* Booster involvement is a direct violation of NCAA rules.

- *Promises of easy admission, "friendly" professors, or easy courses.* Such promises are rarely made to parents or coaches, but they are made to kids. Be sure you talk to your child frequently about his or her conversations with coaches.

6. *Ask the right questions at the right time.* After students visit one or more colleges, they need help making a decision about which of them is the right school for them. Visits are an important part of the college selection process. If the student is highly recruited, these visits may be paid for by the college's athletic department. Even if the student isn't being recruited, visits are recommended, especially if the student plans to play a sport in college.

It's important to recognize that NCAA Division II schools can grant full scholarships, but usually award only partial scholarships. Division III schools, some of the finest colleges and universities in the nation, do not grant scholarships. They provide financial aid and a variety of academic scholarships, but they are not allowed by the NCAA to award athletic scholarships.

Visit with a purpose. When you and your child visit a school to look at its sports program—whether the child expects a scholarship or not—you should have several questions to ask of a variety of people on campus. Review the questions on the following two forms to guide your thinking. They are borrowed from my book, *Advising Student-Athletes Through the College Selection Process,* Prentice Hall, 1996.

Additional Considerations for Female Athletes

Most women's programs in college have very restrictive budgets. Coaches are unable to recruit as broadly or as aggressively as many men's program. This means that recruiting is different for them. Because of this, girls should consider one or more of the following steps which help promote the recruiting process:

1. The athlete should write coaches after the junior year, mentioning educational and athletic accomplishments, awards and honors, and her size.

2. She should ask her coach and/or an opposing coach to write a letter at the same time in which the coach mentions the athlete's desire and unique qualifications to compete on the college level.

3. After hearing from one or more schools, she should call the ones that interest her to ask if the coaches would like to see highlight tapes.

4. During her senior year, she should maintain the interest of coaches by sending occasional letters with newspaper clippings and other indications of academic and athletic progress.

5. At the conclusion of the senior year, she should write another letter, reintroducing herself and expressing her desire to pursue her sport in college.

6. She or, preferably, her coach should make a follow-up phone call to determine if the school would like to see additional highlight tapes.

7. She or her coach should call again in a few weeks after the college coach has had time to evaluate the tapes. If the college is interested in the athlete, arrange for a visit.

It's unfortunate but true that many high school coaches are either unwilling or unable to help their athletes find college programs. Many are intimidated by the process or just don't know what to do. Others simply can't find the time. Unfortunately, there are many coaches in this position, so young athletes and/or their parents find themselves doing most of the leg work. On the other hand, many kids are blessed with coaches who help above and beyond the call of duty. If your child is fortunate enough to have such a coach, have him or her handle most of the previous responsibilities.

The Realities of "Walking On"

Most schools allow selected athletes to "walk on," that is to be on their teams without a scholarship. Such athletes, according to college coaches, are potentially good enough to play for the team, just not good enough at that time to be awarded a scholarship. Walk-on athletes are gifted players in their own right and sometimes earn scholarships after one or two years of participation. Such opportunities, therefore, are not granted to just any athlete. High school coaches must document for colleges a youngster's qualifications to walk on. Most high school coaches are also careful about *where* they try to help their kids walk on.

College coaches tend to recruit the regions around their schools, especially their own states. Because neighboring high schools are so important to them, they establish relationships with the coaches in these schools in order to get the inside track on the recruitment of outstanding athletes.

In order to maintain such relationships, college coaches try to keep the high schools happy, firstly by dealing fairly with any athletes they recruit from the schools and, secondly, by treating walk-ons like any other member of their teams. The young athlete from Wisconsin who wants to walk on at Arizona State may be disappointed to learn about this reality, but he or she is likely to have a better experience at a school in Wisconsin or elsewhere in the Midwest. So be sure to ask your athlete's high school coach to coordinate all contacts and discussions regarding walking on.

Let's Wrap It Up

One of my favorite sportswriters in the Midwest, Taylor Bell, wrote this description in his column a couple years ago:

> "Too slow," college coaches said.
> Notre Dame and Michigan showed
> no interest. He visited Illinois and
> Wisconsin. But they didn't offer a
> scholarship. He chose Purdue because
> he figured to have an opportunity to
> play. And because Purdue was the
> only school that really wanted him.
> "I wanted to prove people wrong.
> My determination came from people
> criticizing me. They didn't think I
> was talented enough to play on the
> college level."

Can you guess who Bell was describing? Mike Alstott, the all-pro fullback/tailback for the Super Bowl champion Tampa Bay Buccaneers. Yes, it's true that Alstott, a future Hall of Famer, wasn't heavily recruited out of high school. And he's certainly not the only player in sports history to prove college recruiters wrong. His story is an inspiration to thousands of kids who realize that hard work and commitment can often overcome any kind of criticism.

So the college scholarship glass is half-full, not half-empty. If your child has set such a goal for herself, tell her to go for it. Just be sure she understands that the path she has chosen is crowded with thousands of other talented youngsters who have set similar goals for themselves. Many are bigger and faster than she is. The child who understands and accepts this reality is happy to take one of several side roads that might lead to a less competitive, and perhaps more enjoyable, level of participation.

7.
DRUGS AND DRINKING

Did You Know?

- Adults who drink excessively can become alcoholics in ten to fifteen years. Teenagers who drink excessively can become alcoholics in six to eighteen *months*!

- Compared with ten to twenty years ago, today's marijuana is ten to twenty times more poisonous to the system.

- Even legal drugs like ephedra have been linked to the deaths of young athletes.

- Crack cocaine can be *immediately* addictive.

- Steroids damage the heart, liver, and reproductive system and provoke extremely violent behavior.

Drugs meet needs, a lot of them. We use them to lower our blood pressure, reduce cholesterol, and combat cancer. They come in handy when we have a headache or an upset stomach. They dull pain, cause weight loss, smooth wrinkles, grow hair, firm up sagging skin, and boost sexual performance. At home, they ease the tensions of the day; at work, they give us energy. Unfortunately, they also inhibit sexual reproduction, damage internal organs, fry brains, and ruin lives.

It seems, then, that the uses of drugs are varied, much like the needs that provoke their use. They make aging less obvious, disease less fatal, stress more tolerable, and pleasure more satisfying. As such, they fill voids in our lives—which is a lot of the problem. Whenever our wants outdistance our needs, we create voids in our lives, then we sometimes go to extremes to fill them. Such extremes are destructive.

What Is Research Telling Us?

Young athletes tend to go to dangerous extremes. Researchers at the University of Pittsburgh interviewed 500 twelve- to sixteen-year-olds in a Pittsburgh-area community who indicated that they did not drink. Just one year later, when reinterviewed, 7 percent of the boys who did not play a team sport said that they were now drinking.

But what about the kids who did play a sport? The percentage changed significantly for them. Of the original group who now played one or two sports, 17 percent were now drinking. And of those who played three sports, 23 percent said that they were now drinking. Also shocking is the fact that they also were involved in more drug use, more violent behavior, and more unprotected sex than their non-athletic schoolmates.

The average age for a youngster's first drink is eleven, and it takes only three to four months for preteens to become alcoholics.

Jerry-Szpak and Brown reported in the *Journal of Child and Adolescent Substance Abuse* that only 14 percent of adolescent athletes in a recent survey described themselves as non-drinkers. How much the other 84 percent drank was not reported, but they all identified themselves as drinkers. In another study, Carr *et al.* reported in the *Journal of Alcohol and Drug Education* that male athletes in their study drank significantly more than male non-athletes, and that male athletes drank to intoxication significantly more often than female athletes.

Studies of college students are just as bad. A recent article in the *Journal of American College Health* reported the results of a survey involving over 51,000 students on 125 campuses. The study was conducted by Southern Illinois University and found that non-athletes averaged 4.12 drinks a week. Athletes averaged 7.34 drinks, and team leaders averaged 8.25. Male athletes averaged about ten drinks a week, while male non-athletes averaged six. What is especially disturbing is that athletes rarely drank during the week, but concentrated most of their drinking at parties after games or on weekend binges.

But let's keep it in perspective. Before I throw a blanket of condemnation over the influence of sports, let's recognize that the aggressive and risk-taking behaviors of many athletes probably would provoke drinking and violence even if they weren't involved in sports. In addition, a youngster's need to "belong" to a team can lead to all kinds of crazy behaviors, including using drugs, binge drinking, even roaming the streets looking for fights. This awareness, however, doesn't get us off the hook.

It's more than the need to belong. Peer pressure is only one problem for young athletes. We've already discussed overexposure to certain sports, abusive or incompetent coaches, a preoccupation with winning, and pressure from friends and family. If coaches are the problem, talk to them or seek remedies by talking to school athletic directors or youth program coordinators. It's also possible that we as parents are part of the problem. Take a quick look in the nearest mirror and if you see someone who may be pressuring your child—*stop*.

Equally important, keep this chapter's statistics in mind. Don't beat your child over the head with them, but recognize that young athletes, especially gifted ones, may be more inclined than their non-athletic classmates to drink and use drugs. Young athletes warrant careful watching. We all keep an eye on our children's curfews, driving skills, study habits, and choice of friends. I suggest the same kind of vigilance, no more no less, with the young athlete(s) in the family.

Tobacco and Alcohol: The Early Culprits

Be especially alert to your child's possible use of tobacco and alcohol. They are insidious killers, and they prove daily that most of us are not as smart as we think we are. How bright can we be, if—worldwide—we consume six million tons of tobacco every year? Does the average smoker display a lot of gray matter when he inhales the toxins in 7,000 cigarettes a year?

3,000 teens and preteens have their first cigarette every day, and one in every five kids in the twelve to seventeen age range smokes.

What makes this especially silly is that smoking is the single biggest killer in this country that *can be stopped*. When we prevent our kids from smoking, therefore, we extend their lives. We also improve their endurance and athletic performance, and we help them observe their athletic program's training rules. Such rules weren't developed by a few old geezers who don't want kids to have fun. They are well-informed and well-intentioned and aim only at the health of young athletes.

Estimates indicate that teenagers buy almost one billion packs of cigarettes every year.

Five more arguments against smoking. If you want to stop your young athlete from smoking, toss these facts into informal conversations with him or her:

1. Nicotine is a poisonous alkaloid. Just a small amount in your bloodstream can kill you in about an hour.

2. A study at the University of Indiana suggested that smokers who average a pack or more a day are 45 percent more likely than non-smokers to use marijuana. This doesn't mean that smoking *causes* marijuana use. It simply suggests a relationship between the two. Mention it this way to your child. Kids are pretty smart. If you argue that smoking *causes* marijuana use, the child probably will know better and might stop listening to all your arguments.

3. Smoking can cause *seventeen* different forms of cancer. This is one argument kids will listen to.

4. Smoking can cause premature wrinkling and significant problems with the stomach and lungs. Young athletes don't worry much about wrinkling, but they are especially sensitive to having problems with the lungs. This argument makes a lot of sense to them.

5. Smokers are *ten times* more likely to get lung cancer than non-smokers.

Compared to the tissues of the lungs, a sheet of tissue paper looks like a sheet of iron.

More About Drinking. No pun intended, but here's a sobering fact. It takes most adults up to fifteen years to become alcoholics. Children? Well, a seventh grader who begins drinking heavily at the beginning of the school year could be an alcoholic during the second semester. The simple reason is that the livers of children are underdeveloped, just one reason why all states have established twenty-one as the legal drinking age. What we tell our children about drinking, therefore, and how we tell it are critical if kids are to develop the self-discipline to avoid behaviors that are so destructive, not only to athletic performance but to lifelong health.

Five Arguments Against Drinking. Smart athletes are winners. We want our kids to have character, be self-disciplined, and consistently commit themselves to their responsibilities as young adults. One of their responsibilities as young athletes is to be at their personal best during practice and contests. This means—*don't drink.* A refusal to drink is a commitment to coaches and teammates, and it has benefits far beyond athletics:

1. Alcohol is involved in 50 percent of all traffic fatalities. One hundred thousand deaths a year are attributed to drinking.

2. More than half the people in this country who are killed in drunk driving incidents are teenagers, even though they account for only 20 percent of all licensed drivers.

3. The only age group in this country whose life expectancy is actually *decreasing* is teenagers. Put it this way with your child. The greatest enemy of today's teenager is today's teenager. They are killing each other in cars, gang fights, and senseless violence whenever they drink too much.

Over half the people killed in drunk driving accidents are teenagers, and they represent only 20 percent of all drivers.

---

4. At any one time in this country, one of every ten people is dependent on alcohol. Even more startling is the fact that one in *four* is dependent at some time in their lives. Such dependence can lead to impotence and infertility, birth defects, and diminished immunity to disease.

5. Be sure to let your child know if someone in your family is alcohol dependent. People with a family history of alcoholism are at risk before the age of twenty. For that matter, studies show that *any* child who begins drinking in adolescence is at risk—family history or not.

In summary, here are five warning signs of alcohol use:

1. slurred speech,

2. unsteady walk,

3. slowed reflexes,

4. relaxed inhibitions,

5. glazed eyes.

A Few Words About Marijuana

Tobacco and alcohol are probably the biggest problems with kids, but marijuana is a very close third. Think about this. A recent study indicates that approximately half of our nation's twelve- to seventeen-year-olds see nothing wrong with using marijuana. They have simply accepted it as a run-of-the-mill recreational drug. This is a very disturbing statistic to those of us who recognize the many dangers associated with the use of marijuana.

Several years ago, some parents I worked with lost their son to a drug overdose. He had been mixing alcohol and marijuana at a party with some friends. None of the kids realized that pot inhibits the body's ability to reject toxic substances. He was unable to throw up after drinking too much alcohol. The combination of the two eventually killed him.

One of my co-authors on an earlier book is an athletic director in a prominent Chicago-area high school. She insists that drug abuse is an epidemic in this country. She is convinced, for example, that marijuana use has become so prominent in our society that many of us no longer question its use.

Many of us have allowed marijuana to become culturally acceptable; others of us have grown so war-weary that we make comments like "Thank heavens it's only pot."

Be careful! Such complacency on the part of adults is deadly. We must continue to fight the good fight. After all, how many kids understand that today's marijuana is ten to twenty times more toxic than the marijuana of the '60s and '70s? Let's not forget earlier statistics indicating that multi-sport athletes are more inclined than non-athletes to use drugs, drink to excess, or engage in violent behavior. These are the very kids who are most likely to use marijuana and to be excused for it because they're "good kids."

Five Arguments Against Marijuana Use

1. One joint of marijuana contains as many as 421 different chemicals. When lit, it contains more than 2,000! Maybe that's why recent studies indicate that one joint can damage the lungs as much as 100 cigarettes. This is an upsetting statistic, not only to parents but to young athletes. Fortunately, more and more kids today are conscious of what they put into their bodies. This statistic gets their attention.

2. Marijuana is fat soluble, which means that the body doesn't eliminate it quickly. In fact, one joint is stored in the body from one to three weeks. This means that even one joint a day can cause an accumulation of enough toxic substances to severely damage the brain and the entire respiratory system. This is a sobering fact to most kids, but it is especially

startling to young athletes who strive for peak performance.

3. Children are 104 times more likely to use cocaine if they smoke marijuana.

4. The accumulation of toxic substances in the body caused by regular marijuana use kills brain cells and causes changes that make dependency on other drugs more likely. In fact, kids who use drugs early in life invariably end up in drug treatment programs.

5. The average age for first use of marijuana is fourteen, and research reveals that one in every four eighth-graders has used marijuana at least once.

Recent studies indicate that awareness of statistics on the danger of marijuana use among college students have led to a decline in use by 35 percent to 40 percent.

Here are five warning signs of marijuana use:

1. dry mouth,

2. excitement, laughter,

3. red eyes,

4. increased hunger,

5. also watch for rolling paper, pipes, and the odor of burned hemp rope.

The Case Against Cocaine and Other Drugs

Because of its expense, cocaine use is rare among youngsters. Its popularity within the rest of society, however, is alarming. Estimates indicate that at least five thousand people try cocaine for the first time each day. Its temptation involves not only feelings of well-being, but the false sense of status of being one of society's "movers and shakers." Cocaine use is associated with "upward mobility" and with success in the corporate and financial worlds.

"Freebased" cocaine—cocaine that can be smoked—is called "crack." "Crack" cocaine, on the other hand, is easily available to youngsters. In fact, drug dealers often give it to children for free to "hook" them so that they will continue needing it. In many instances, crack cocaine is immediately addictive. It is also relatively inexpensive. Some kids use it only a few times and need it from then on.

Here are five arguments against cocaine use:

1. Crack cocaine is made in basements, crack houses, anywhere that is secret and inexpensive. Gang members who make it are more concerned about privacy than cleanliness.

2. In addition to the unhealthy effects on users, cocaine—when injected—involves the risk of infection with HIV and AIDS.

3. As indicated already, crack cocaine can be immediately addictive. Users of crack can never be sure if the next dose will cause addiction or even death.

4. Because crack cocaine has strong ties to gangs, youngsters often take their lives in their hands even when they buy it. The media are full of stories of youngsters who have been killed in inner city neighborhoods when trying to buy drugs. Then, if the child becomes addicted, he or she is likely to become a gang member or a prostitute to support the habit.

5. Be honest with your child during discussions of drug use. Cocaine *does* create momentary happiness. But be sure the child also realizes that it is also followed by sudden and often severe depression, the kind that sometimes requires the help of psychiatrists.

Four warning signs of cocaine use are:

1. restlessness,

2. increased excitement,

3. manic behavior,

4. also watch for glass vials, glass pipes, razor blades, syringes, and needle marks on arms.

The more you know, the safer your child. Other drugs may affect your young athlete as well. The more you know about their characteristics and warning signs, the less likely your child will be to use drugs. This is especially true if your child knows that you know about these drugs, especially the warning signs. For that reason I've provided a one-page summary of drugs and their warning signs.

The value of such a summary is that it enables athletes to recognize the signs of drug use in their teammates or friends and to reach out to them. It emphasizes that friends don't let friends use life-threatening substances. It also proves to children that *you* know all the signs of drug use and that you're *watching*. Vince Lombardi once said, "Discipline is part of the will, really. A disciplined person is one who follows the will of the one who gives the orders." I submit that if your child abides by your expectations often enough, self-discipline results.

Facts About Other Drugs

Some drugs are much less prevalent among kids but are dangerous enough to warrant mention.

Depressants. Depressants reduce sensitivity to stimulation, which makes them desirable to kids who are nervous, very self-conscious, or generally fearful. They relax and promote self-confidence, but they also cause depression and weight loss. These aspects are bad enough for young athletes, but some depressants can also result in overdose as well as in hepatitis or AIDS due to the use of unsterile needles.

Inhalants. Varnish, lighter fluid, airplane glue, hair spray, even typewriter correction fluid can make some kids "high." Such inhalants are easily accessible. Be sure to identify their warning signs and to be especially vigilant if you fear that your child may be tempted to use such substances.

Hallucinogens. Drugs such as LSD, peyote, mescaline, and PCP are strong stimulants that increase brain activity and result in altered perceptions of reality. Hallucinogens create an immediate sense of euphoria but also can cause flashbacks, which often result in terrifying reactions, sometimes well after the use of

185

the drug. PCP often results in serious injury or death because the behavior of users becomes bizarre and violent.

Stimulants. The parents of young athletes should also be familiar with methamphetamines. Commonly called "speed," "crystal," or "crank" on the street, methamphetamines stimulate the senses. Some young athletes believe that it increases their reaction time and improves their athletic skills, but most often all it leads to is severe anxiety. When its chemical structure is modified, it results in a drug called "ecstasy." Like cocaine, ecstasy is made in underground labs with no concern for cleanliness.

Warning Signs of the Use of These Drugs:

- *Depressants*—Lack of coordination, drowsiness, confusion, and slurred speech.

- *Inhalants*—Nausea, dizziness, poor coordination and muscle control, and headaches.

- *Hallucinogens*—Anxiety, panic, and nausea. Also watch for such things as capsules, tablets, and blotter squares.

- *Stimulants*—Irritability, sweating, nausea, palpitations, and high blood pressure.

The What and Why of Steroids

Consider these stories. A young football player in the Midwest died recently of a heart attack, the result of a diseased and enlarged heart. The puncture wounds in the youngster's thighs and the atrophying of his testicles convinced the county coroner that steroids killed him. He had collapsed during practice and died later in the hospital.

About the same time, a football player from the SEC (Southeast Conference) discussed his use of anabolic steroids and his subsequent aggressiveness and thoughts of suicide. Years earlier, in a passionate and dramatic admission, the late Lyle Alzado vowed that his own abuse of steroids caused his cancer and enlarged heart. Both athletes admitted their violent behavior resulting from "roid rages" and warned young athletes that nothing in sports warrants the possible self-destruction caused by steroids.

The problem is virtually everywhere. What is alarming to most of us is that steroid use is widespread among athletes at all levels of competition. It is perhaps most prevalent among elite and professional athletes, but they're not the only ones with a lot riding on superior performance. In spite of media claims to the contrary, money is not an athlete's most important motivator. Every athlete at every level—and this is especially true of young athletes—is more concerned about the needs to be recognized, to achieve, to give expression to the demands of his or her talent, and to find the satisfactions of hard work and maximum effort.

Many of them believe that steroids will satisfy these needs. What is tragic is that sometimes they do. Steroids *can* improve their performance and achievement and result in broader recognition. They also can promote and enhance the expression of natural talent. As such, they can lead to college scholarships, professional contracts, and fame and fortune. The challenges facing coaches and parents, therefore, are enormous.

How widespread is the use of steroids? Experts estimate that anywhere from 15 percent to 80 percent of NFL players have used steroids. It's not surprising, perhaps, that the low end of the range is reported by the players themselves, the higher end by sports psychologists and medical personnel. A few years ago, estimates indicated that 60 percent to 80 percent of the world's elite athletes have used steroids. That number has declined, significantly in some sports, because of the effectiveness of drug testing. Even testers will admit, however, that their procedures are not foolproof because of the availability of drugs that camouflage steroids in the blood.

According to the **Chicago Tribune,** *"[One player] alleged that at least half of major league players use steroids in an attempt to gain muscle strength and bulk. Upon his retirement earlier this month, [another player] told reporters he believes the number is as high as 85 percent."*

Steroids are used in youth sports and by junior and senior highs students, too. Of particular concern to the parents of high school and junior high school athletes are the claims of many sports psychologists and doctors that as many as half a million junior high school and secondary school athletes could be using steroids to improve their appearance and athletic performance. Recent studies as reported in the *Journal of Pediatrics* indicate that children as young as ten are using steroids. Size and general appearance are concerns to them, too. Steroids represent a quick fix.

> *A recent survey, as reported in the* Chicago Sun-Times, *indicates "that 2.7 percent of 965 youngsters questioned at four Massachusetts middle schools are using anabolic steroids. Experts said that represents a significant problem."*

Five Warning Signs of Steroid Use:

1. acne,

2. significant weight gain,

3. altered moods, especially increased anger,

4. facial puffiness,

5. hair loss in males—increased facial hair and deeper voice in females.

Even Legal Drugs Can Be Harmful

Consider the recent problems with ephedrine, an over-the-counter drug that, within the past ten years, has resulted in seventeen deaths. Recently, a professional baseball player and a college football player died from ephedrine-related complications. The drug was not blamed exclusively in either instance, but it was mentioned prominently as a contributing factor.

Ephedrine is reported to relieve bronchial asthma, but it also increases heart rate and blood pressure. Because it is used by athletes to enhance performance and lose weight, it is especially dangerous if used to excess. This is the primary reason why the Federal Drug Administration (FDA) recommends that ephedrine-containing products warn users that exceeding recommended dosages may result in heart attack, stroke, or seizure.

What about creatine supplements? Found naturally in meat and fish, creatine is available in supplemental form, but has not been approved by the FDA. It is used by athletes to promote muscle mass and strength gains and does, in fact, seem to benefit such explosive exercises. But it does little for aerobic strength or endurance. In fact, researchers are convinced that the bulk provided by creatine is nothing more than water retention in the muscle. The jury is still out on the benefits of creatine.

What researchers *do* know is that anyone under the age of sixteen should not use creatine. Because its effects are still being studied by the FDA and other medical researchers, no one in the medical community is willing to rule out potentially dangerous side effects.

A friend told to me the other day that his nephew, a freshman athlete in high school, asked his coach how he could gain weight. The coach recommended creatine, even told the boy that he would get some for him. Fortunately, my friend—a long-time coach—intervened.

Where are the role models? Well, most of them are professional athletes, and a lot of them model all the wrong things. The coach in the previous story is another such example. Today's kids are influenced by growing numbers of trash-talking, chest-bumping brats who jump higher, run faster, and hit harder than their earlier college and professional counterparts and who become millionaires almost as soon as they learn to make the rest of us slack-jawed by the sheer brilliance of their athletic performances.

Many of them also stun us with their aberrant behavior, personal appearance, drug usage, and bizarre and excessive lifestyles. Unfortunately, their athletic talents and their evident financial success make them role models for large numbers of kids. Because kids admire such athletes, they regard sports as the yellow-brick road to similar fame and fortune and see nothing wrong with using drugs. Our job as parents is to set such kids straight, to help them develop the self-discipline and the character so lacking in the athletes they seek to emulate.

So what do we do? First of all, we learn more about the harmful effects of drug use. Many parents are unfamiliar with the terrible dangers of teenage drinking. Some actually allow drinking at parties in the home, particularly after games, in order to be "friends" to their children. Others fail to discipline with the consistency and the severity that some children require. Let's never forget that children expect and *want* boundaries. To quote John Wooden's philosophy again, "Make the rules clear and the penalties severe."

Certainly, Wooden would never promote unfair boundaries or unreasonable punishments. Nor would he ever disregard the needs of youngsters, but he did believe that self-discipline grows in a caring and consistent environment that is intolerant of chronic and destructive misbehavior. He would be among the first to agree with the following suggestions to parents:

- Learn all the signs of drug use and watch your young athlete carefully. Even the best kids from the best families occasionally give in to temptation.

- Have "zero tolerance" for drug use and apply consequences fairly and consistently. Be sure to outline such consequences before the fact so that there is no disagreement between you and your child if consequences are warranted.

What about telling them to just say no? "Just say no?" It's good advice, but let's be realistic. "Just say no" is an appealing slogan and seems to push kids in the right direction, but it misses a fundamental point. Kids who can "Just say no" are already self-disciplined. Most of their personal and social needs have been satisfied, and they have developed the self-criticism, moral reflection, and self-discipline that make saying no quite simple. It isn't that easy for most other kids.

Peer pressure, pressure for grades, pressure to win, pressure from parents, pressure from the local gang, pressure to wear the right clothes, live in the right house, and drive the right car all conspire against kids and inhibit their ability to just say no. As a result, cheating is a growing problem in classrooms; winning at all costs is a problem in sports; escalating violence is a problem in our schools; and drug abuse is a problem in every corner of our communities.

What is most important is that you just say no. "Just say no" is still good advice for most kids, but until they learn how to do it, parents will have to say no for and to them. Create self-discipline in your child by helping develop the character that makes saying no easier. Such character is developed by teaching them appropriate values and behavior, then by expecting them to behave accordingly. It's one thing for kids to know the right thing to do; it's another for them to actually do it.

Kids learn to say no for a variety of reasons. They know that drugs are a health hazard. Drugs also inhibit athletic performance. Be sure to emphasize this with your young athlete. You and I understand that good health is the most obvious reason to stay away from drugs. But, unlike most teenagers, we no longer entertain expectations of immortality. Thoughts that they're going to live forever tend to close kids' minds to common sense issues like good health.

Concern about athletic performance is another issue. While "Damage my brain cells" may seem an abstract possibility, ruining a jump shot, screwing up a swing, or destroying the ability to find open receivers is a little something in the here and now that will get a child's attention. So talk about both issues, problems with health *and* performance. The impact on kids will be more pronounced.

Seven Characteristics of Peak Performance

A short time ago, a variety of accomplished athletes were asked to describe themselves when they were performing at their absolute best. "When you are at peak performance, how do you feel? What's going on in your head?" They identified seven characteristics: no fear of failure, performance more important than outcome, complete focus on execution of skills, effortlessness, a feeling of complete control, good time/space orientation, and positive thinking.

Drugs destroy such peak performance. Discuss this fact with your child. When you do, use the following information to point out the negative effects of drug use on peak performance:

1. *Self-confidence and no fear of failure.* Drug users have little self-confidence and usually realize even less success. In fact, their fear of failure is one of the biggest reasons for their use of drugs. So let your child know that using drugs is a sure sign of weakness.

2. *Performance more important than outcome.* Athletes who are focused on their performance are more concerned with "What am I doing and how well am I doing it?" than with "Am I winning?" Most kids who use drugs use them because they're afraid to lose. They have almost a total preoccupation with winning. Remember: *The outcome of the game—winning—is always less important than the child's effort and his or her focus on performance.*

3. *Complete focus on execution of skills.* Stimulants, depressants, and other drugs destroy focus. It is virtually impossible for drug users to focus on anything, let alone the execution of their athletic skills.

The manager of a major league baseball team, as quoted in the **Chicago Tribune:** *"I remember in the '70s that cocaine was prevalent. When a guy missed a ball in the field or staggered around on a fly ball, everyone accused him of being on drugs. That's almost thirty years ago, and we're still going through almost the same thing. We're going to have to sit down and find a solution to it."*

---

4. Effortless performance. Athletes who are experiencing peak performance don't force anything. They are "in the flow," performing effortlessly. Some young athletes believe that depressants might help in this area. In reality, depressants bring kids down

too far—to the point where focus and general performance are hurt.

5. *Being in complete control of all faculties.* The answer to this one is obvious. Once a child ingests drugs, the drugs take control. Physical skills surrender to the effects of the drug. In fact, drugs often create a feeling of being *out* of control.

6. *Good time/space orientation.* Athletes who are at peak performance actually slow down time. They "see" everything around them while performing their skills. Like Greg Louganis or any other elite diver, they know exactly where they are in space during every twist and turn. Drugs destroy this ability.

A friend's football team was losing a championship game a few years ago. His quarterback, usually pretty good, was having a terrible day. In a desperate attempt to win the game, he threw the ball far downfield, overthrowing a double-covered receiver in the end zone. The game ended, the teams congratulated each other, and my friend's team, heads hanging, crossed the field for their locker room.

But that was not the end of the story. The next day, my friend was reviewing the game tape and discovered that his quarterback's primary receiver on the final play of the game was wide open in the end zone—even waving his arms. As he tells the story, he just shook his head and chalked up the quarterback's panic to the pressure of the game. He didn't find out until many years later that his quarterback and seven or eight other kids on the team had used amphetamines just before the game to get "fired up."

What his kids didn't know was that amphetamines may elevate mood and alertness and increase self-confidence, but they also distort the user's perception of reality and impair judgment. The result was that his quarterback's perceptions were going *too fast*. He was unable to slow down time and gain the self-control he needed to find his receiver in the end zone. Expecting heightened alertness and improved performance, here was a young man who was seeing things too quickly and who lost the game for his team.

Positive thinking. Young athletes who think positively expect only the best. They don't worry about failure. But how can kids think positively about their performance when stimulants damage their lungs and depressants destroy their reflexes? Children who think positively and who put winning in perspective don't need drugs.

Let's Wrap It Up

We owe our kids a whole lot more than a drive to and from practice. As parents, we owe them the benefit of our experience and the occasional push that promotes not only an understanding of drug use, but the behaviors that lead to self-discipline and character development. Self-disciplined kids have character, and kids with character don't need drugs. Let's admit it, they may experiment occasionally, but they don't require the drug-induced relief that soothes chronic emotional pain.

But we don't want them to experiment either. Experimentation may be a reality in our society only because it signals the absence of *something* in the lives of our kids. Teenagers can do some pretty crazy things, and drug experimentation is only one of them, but we still can't accept such a behavior, no matter how developmentally predictable it may seem. Kids need adults in their lives who regard drug use and other self-destructive behaviors as black and white issues. Unlike many other segments of our society, dedicated parents have the strength of character to say yes or no to kids.

I look back periodically on my experiences as a high school and college athlete and thank heaven above that I worked with coaches who had little tolerance for my stupidity. Winners aren't stupid or undisciplined. It's that simple. And our job as parents is to develop winners, not just winning programs for local coaches. Winning is a state of mind, not numbers on a scoreboard. Kids who make a maximum effort, who work hard to develop character may lose their share of games, but they're going to win more than their share of life's battles.

When *winning* is the exclusive focus of our sports programs and of our expectations at home, and when each kid's efforts never seem to relieve his *need* to win, kids lose self-discipline and the ability to just say no. In an ideal world, where the thrill of participation and a maximum effort are their own rewards—even in a losing cause—drugs are unnecessary. Personally fulfilled youngsters don't need performance enhancing drugs or mind-numbing escapes from the reality of their daily lives.

Finally, be careful how you use the statistics in this chapter. Statistics are useful because they show relationships. Unfortunately, the media often use them for shock value, suggesting that the statistic involves causality.

If you tell your child that smoking leads to marijuana use, which leads to cocaine use, which leads to addiction, you might be on shaky ground.

Her experiences with friends who smoke might prove otherwise.

If she discovers that any of your advice or concerns are mistaken—or if your comments are used for shock value—she will stop listening to you. Don't take that chance; use these statistics carefully. Most important, use them to talk to your child. Keep the lines of communication open. Parents who routinely talk to their children about such important issues as drugs provide information, a sense of caring, and—most important—the opportunity for the children to reflect on the consequences of decisions they have made or are about to make. Kids are inclined to do the right thing, especially once they hear themselves committing to it.

8.
SUCCESS STORIES AND WORDS OF WISDOM

Do You Know Who Said It?

- "You have to have some dislike for your opponent if you're going to win a championship."

- "Every time you win, you're reborn; when you lose, you die a little."

- "Winning isn't everything; the will to win is everything. It is more important than any event that occasions it."

The first quote came from basketball great Earvin "Magic" Johnson, the second from coaching legend George Allen. Both men influenced their sports as much as anyone in professional sports history. Maybe they accurately reflect the opinions and attitudes of most professional athletes and coaches. Maybe such thoughts are motivating for them and bring out their best during competition.

They don't reflect the thinking of all professionals, however, because the third quote belongs to coaching great Vince Lombardi. Often misquoted as saying "Winning isn't everything; it's the only thing," Lombardi was convinced that not only did losing *not* involve dying a little, it provided opportunities for learning and for a recommitment to the *will* to win.

Lombardi's philosophy of competition is appropriate for every level of competition, youth to professional.

Maybe the first two quotes are okay for the pros, but they're clearly out of place in amateur competition, even in college. Such emphases on winning disregard traditional notions of respect for one's opponent and the simple pleasures found in participation for its own sake. "Dislike of your opponent" and "Dying a little every time you lose" transform athletic competition into a thoughtless disregard of everything good in sports and create a stressful and destructive preoccupation with winning.

Let's admit it, winning—sometimes at all costs—is the ultimate goal of more and more people across the country, from Little League to big league, many using strategies ranging from college quick openers to corporate power plays. Money is probably the biggest reason, but to blame it all on money is to overlook a variety of subtle yet powerful influences on all of us. "Beating the other guy" is a virus that infects school class rank, our choice of clothes and cars, even our driving habits.

But it wasn't always like that. Travel back in time for a moment to the late 1800s, to a time when professional baseball was in its infancy, when the words, "It's not whether you win or lose but how you play that game that counts," were more than a reminder of early American naiveté. In 1845 Alexander Cartwright laid out the dimensions of the first "base ball" field, and shortly afterward, in 1860, the fathers of the game established rules like:

- The umpire ensures that the game is played in a gentlemanly manner.

- The umpire may also ask ballists (players) and spectators for help in making decisions.

- The ball is tossed underhanded as closely as possible to where the striker (batter) desires it.

- Speed balls or other intentionally deceptive pitching is forbidden and considered ungentlemanly.

Times have changed, haven't they? And not all the changes have been good. It's not uncommon now to see baseball players sliding spikes first into a second baseman to break up a double play or for pitchers to throw fast balls at batters' heads to back them away from the plate. Baseball players are now getting higher salaries for lower batting averages and are pumping themselves up with steroids instead of pride. The worst part of all this is that it's infectious. Kids pick up on the same behaviors, so do you and I.

Four Important Principles

So how do we return to a time when ballists throw gentlemanly pitches and umpires ask spectators for help making decisions? That will never happen, but we can do more than we're doing. Let's start by contrasting Johnson's and Allen's quotes with four of the most important principles emphasized in this book. Then consider related quotes from solid thinkers like Lombardi:

1. *Emphasize performance over outcome in just about everything kids do.* When kids think positively about hard work, maximum effort, cooperation with others, and focused and consistent performance, the outcome of the task is less important to them. In

fact, the outcome usually takes care of itself when the child's focus is on maximum performance.

"Things may come to those who wait, but only the things left by those who hustle."
—*Abraham Lincoln*

"Life doesn't mean money. It doesn't mean success. It just means doing things as well as you can without worrying about anything else."
—*Terry Fox*

"The only thing I ever thought about was to be as good as I could. I never thought about being the greatest baseball player or anything, just to be as good as I could."
—*Hank Aaron*

"My only goal is to raise the level of my performance."
—*Greg Louganis*

---

2. *Losing can be good.* It's our best chance to learn. We all make mistakes—in just about everything we do. The smart ones among us learn from our mistakes so we don't make them again. We also learn to seek experiences with some risk of defeat because we realize that such risks lead to growth and improvement. Parents and coaches must teach these important lessons to kids.

"What is defeat? Nothing but education, nothing but the first step toward something better."
—*Wendell Phillips*

"Success is not forever, and failure isn't fatal."
—*Don Shula*

"Find out what you don't do well, then don't do it."
—*Yogi Berra*

3. *Kids must want to win—never need to win.* The key to any success is consistent and maximum effort, as Vince Lombardi said, having the *will* to win. The will to perform well is more important than the outcome of that performance. Kids who will to win are cooperative, learn their assignments, take advice, and make maximum efforts—all the time. Kids who *need* to win—when their focus is only on outcome—may not make maximum efforts. Instead, they may cheat or just give up. We want our children to work hard for their victories. We never want winning to be so important that they'll lie or cheat to achieve it.

"The harder you work, the harder it is to lose."
—*Vince Lombardi*

"The people most preoccupied with titles and status are usually the least deserving of them."
—*Anonymous*

"The best way to make your dreams come true is to wake up."
—*J. M. Power*

"Praise is like poison. It can't hurt you unless you swallow it."
—*Joe Paterno*

4. *Positive thinking creates; negative thinking destroys.* We must help young people think positively about themselves and others. Positive thinking enhances performance and avoids burnout. When kids—when any of us—think negatively, we usually bring about the things we most fear. The child who thinks only about missing the free throw or dropping the pass will miss the free throw and drop the pass. Quantum scientists are correct when they tell us that we create what we think. Youngsters who think positive thoughts invariably have good things happen to them.

"No one makes you feel inferior without your consent."
—*Eleanor Roosevelt*

"Always do what you are afraid to do."
—*Ralph Waldo Emerson*

"Second place is meaningless. You can't always be first, but you have to believe you should have been—that you were never beaten—that time just ran out on you."
—*Vince Lombardi*

"The block of granite which is an obstacle in the pathway of the weak, becomes a stepping-stone in the pathway of the strong."
—*Thomas Carlyle*

"Either I will find a way or I will make one."
—*Philip Sidney*

A Word of Warning

A long-time coach and athletic director in a major metropolitan area was recently interviewed in one of the city's leading newspapers. To quote him: "Values aren't there. In the past, kids would listen, make sense of things, and do what they had to do to be successful. Now it is like talking to a wall. They think they know better than coaches who have been around for ten or fifteen years." He went on to indicate that kids' priorities are out of order: "They settle for the streets. They don't develop all aspects of their personalities or define broad enough goals to be successful in life."

In essence, their focus on sports leaves little room for academics. One result is that, in a recent year, only three public league basketball players in the entire city, one of the two or three largest in the nation, met the NCAA eligibility requirements to play for Division I schools. Said the coach: "Emphasis on academics has deteriorated, along with respect, integrity, discipline, and other values."

So what are some of the solutions? "Just putting money and ideas out there isn't enough. What has to happen is in the trenches, in the elementary schools. The kids have to be advised of what they have to do when they get to high school so it will be meaningful," the coach suggested.

Good advice. What form does it have to take? Certainly, it must involve commitment. Vince Lombardi, as quoted earlier in this chapter, suggested that the purpose of any competition—whether it be field hockey, checkers, or tic-tac-toe—is not just to win but to make the effort to win. Young athletes who learn this lesson early in life become success stories, whether they are starters or members of the supporting cast. What is key is that they make commitments to work hard and to behave like winners. The child who behaves like a winner long enough eventually becomes a winner.

Please excuse the dust covering this phrase, but hard work really is its own reward. Youngsters who accept it and find pleasure in it do wonderful things in life. They may not make the traveling team in Little League, play in many games in junior high, or become all-conference players in high school, but the values they learn in the process influence them for the rest of their lives. All coaches and parents must learn this lesson. It represents the very essence of our relationships with young athletes.

Reasons to Be Hopeful

A few success stories prove the point. Athletic competition can be among the most significant influences in a child's life. Associations with coaches, other athletes, even fans can provide the direction many kids need. The following stories illustrate this. The first two are borrowed from a major metropolitan newspaper. The names and circumstances of the stories have been changed to maintain the anonymity of the athletes. The third story involves a friend of mine, in fact, two friends of mine. It's one of my favorite stories.

Rory. Rory is his high school's leading scorer. He attributes his success to his height—6'7"—and to his hustle—virtually unlimited. Rory has been hustling since the middle of his freshman year in high school when he left a home overcrowded with his sister and her three children and moved into an apartment with four friends. "Hustle" also helps him support himself by working seven days a week as a concessions worker in a local theater, sometimes until after midnight. Rarely does he start his schoolwork before then.

Said his coach about Rory: "He used to really get angry, he'd throw anything in sight and thunder off the floor." This uncontrolled anger caused Rory to be suspended from school, even to end up in the hospital because of fights. Said Rory, "I'd go looking for fights. I've had broken bones, scratches, cuts. I'd go home, clean myself up and get something to eat."

He used to blame his parents for much of his anger. "In eighth grade, my father told me he wished I wasn't born." But his coach convinced him that his anger was his own fault and that he could control it if he tried hard enough. He also learned to control his schoolwork and to think about his future. In essence, his coach taught Rory *to think positively*, to believe in himself, to take responsibility for his own behavior, and to expect good things from his future.

The coach's influence on Rory was profound. He taught Rory to forget outcomes and *to focus on performance*, not only on the basketball court but in the classroom and on the streets after work. Rory's class work improved, and he stopped fighting. Reflecting about his coach and the influence he had on his life, Rory said: "I still get mad, but now I know what to do about it. I really believe now that I control my own future, so I watch myself."

Andy. Andy attended a school representing both ends of the economic scale. Andy was on the lower end, living with his mother and her boyfriend in a neighborhood where the battle against poverty rang out with occasional gunshots. Said Andy, "You don't want to hang out there. It just isn't very good for your health."

Because his mother worked most of the time and his father had left home when Andy was only 5, Andy started getting into trouble at a very early age. He drank, used drugs, and stayed out late. Every time he came home late, he fought with his mom. Andy would storm out of the house and return two or three days later. "There was a time when I was angry and I thought I hated my mom," he said. "I look back at it now and think, 'She did the best she could do.'"

Through sports, Andy found himself. Not only is he the star performer on his school's track team, but he recently finished second in his state's wrestling championships. Andy was also found by a local businessman who has entered his life by rewarding him for his grades and school attendance. Andy's new sponsor has even promised to pay for Andy's college education if he continues to do well in school. Andy had four A's and a B on a recent report card.

Says Andy: "Are you kidding? I get paid for this now. If I keep this up, I can go to college for free." He also adds: "Sometimes I look back and wonder what it would be like if I didn't have sports or this guy in my life. I'd probably be out stealing or selling drugs."

Maggie. I met Maggie when she was a freshman in high school, her coach was a good friend of mine. Her dad had deserted the family when she was only four, and her mom, although concerned about her kids, worked nights and rarely saw them. Two of Maggie's three older sisters had children out of wedlock and still weren't married. One was an addict and had moved to the inner city. As far as Maggie knew, she was walking the streets.

Her coach and I could only imagine how Maggie developed a love of volleyball, but she did. She tried out for and made the team every year, but she rarely played. By Maggie's own admission: "Someone has to sit on the end of the bench and stop it from sliding away. That's my job and I'm good at it." But Maggie's coach loved her and managed to find time for her just about every day. Maggie would come to her office, or the coach would meet Maggie in the school library to check on her homework.

With the coach's help, Maggie started believing in herself, even planning on college after graduation. Said Maggie, "She really made me think I could do my class work, and you know what? I did do it. Just like volleyball—she told me to concentrate on the fundamentals and the grades would take care of themselves. Well, I sat on the bench in volleyball, but I sure became a player in the classroom!"

Maggie did go to college. With her coach's and counselor's help, she received a generous financial aid package to attend a local university. At last word, she was playing intramural volleyball and majoring in English—planning to be a teacher. Ralph Waldo Emerson said it: "You cannot do a kindness too soon, for you never know how soon it will be too late." Coaches have such opportunities every day. The good ones take advantage of them.

Jim. A few years ago, Jim was hired as the head

football coach in an inner city high school. The school was populated by gifted young athletes, but rarely did the football team have a winning record. Many of the best players either dropped out of school or became academically ineligible by their junior or senior years.

During his first year at the school, Jim organized what he called an "Athletic Study Hall." It was designed for kids on his team who received notices of unsatisfactory progress in any of their classes or who were identified by teachers as needing extra help. Players assigned to it were required to attend forty-five minutes before school started, and each was assigned to a tutor who helped the athlete with class assignments and explanations of course work.

Jim knew that the members of the National Honor Society were required to do volunteer work, so he asked them to provide the tutoring. The Athletic Study Hall became a resounding success. Not only did many of Jim's players stay in school and maintain their athletic eligibility, but his team won more games and many of his kids went on to college or trade school after graduation. The school even started a similar program for the general student population, calling it the Rise and Shine Tutoring Program.

Our schools are full of magical ideas just waiting for creative and caring people to uncover them. Jim is one such person. He summed up his program in a recent conversation: "The program sure helped my football team. Most of the good athletes stayed in school until graduation, so our won-loss record really improved. But you know what? Watching kids who earlier might have dropped out walk across that stage at the end of the school year and pick up a diploma made all of us winners—for a whole lot longer than one football season."

Everyone must make a commitment. Here's a coach who's willing to make a commitment, not just to a team but to every youngster on the team. Sure, he realizes that if he can keep his best athletes eligible, his team will win more games. But he also realizes that the team will be a winner only when every player on it is a winner. "Winners win." Good coaches make such commitments to their athletes—all the time.

Said Vince Lombardi: "The great hope of society is individual character. If you would create something, you must first be something."

To paraphrase Lombardi, to accomplish something worthwhile, we must be something worthwhile. That is the primary job of every parent and coach— to be something special and to help their kids feel and be something special. Special parents and coaches model special behaviors, and special kids do special things. What results is mutual commitment. Youngsters commit to the hard work and self-sacrifice required of them, and parents and coaches commit not only to the athletic but to the personal and social development of their kids.

When commitment is made visible. Obviously, talking about commitment is one thing; acting on our commitments is another. After all, character is not only knowing the right thing to do—but doing it. To help folks involved in the athletic program make such commitments, it's a good idea to explain what is expected of them before the season even starts. The best way to do that is with the attached pledges. Each pledge outlines the expected behaviors of athletes, coaches, and parents and asks them to make a commitment by signing the form. These pledges were borrowed from two of my earlier books, *Building the Total Athlete* and *The Athletic Director's Survival Guide* (both published by Prentice Hall). They have been modified to fit the needs of this book.

Said Ralph Waldo Emerson: "What you do speaks so loud that I cannot hear what you say."

The Athlete's Pledge

1. To abide by school and community expectations of my behavior.

2. To follow the training rules.

3. To work hard in practice.

4. To attend every practice unless excused by my coach.

5. To emphasize academics and family over athletics.

6. To be a supportive, cooperative, and respectful teammate.

7. To express myself intelligently and appropriately.

8. To understand that winners don't brag and losers don't make excuses.

I accept the above responsibilities.

_____

Athlete's Signature

The Coach's Pledge

1. To be a model of adult behavior.

2. To dignify my athletes as individuals.

3. To expect no more of my athletes than each is capable of.

4. To help each athlete realize his or her full potential.

5. To recognize the primary importance of school and family.

6. To recognize performance as more important than winning or losing.

7. To keep up-to-date on coaching strategy.

8. To be available to parents whenever mutually convenient.

9. To work with other school personnel to assure the best for my athletes.

I accept the above responsibilities.

_____

Coach's Signature

The Parent's Pledge

1. To attend as many informational meetings as possible.

2. To work closely with coaches and others to assure good academic as well as athletic experiences for my child.

3. To assure that my child will attend all practices and contests.

4. To require my child to abide by training rules.

5. To accept the authority of the coach to determine strategy and player selection.

6. To promote mature behavior from everyone during contests.

7. To work closely with coaches and others to maintain an excellent athletic program.

8. To work with coaches and others to plan my child's future.

I accept the above responsibilities.

_____

Parent's Signature

When we agree before the fact, it's harder to disagree after the fact. The child who agrees not to swear on the field before he gets angry is less likely to swear when he drops a pass. The parent who agrees not to criticize his child's play at any time during the contest is less likely to chastise her when she strikes out. And the coach who agrees before he gets angry not to berate a child on the sidelines is less likely to humiliate the child who forgets an assignment during a game.

And if the child does swear, the parent criticizes, or the coach screams, it's a whole lot easier for us to discuss these behaviors with them if they've signed the pledge. In fact, I've seen parents, coaches, and athletes apologize for such behaviors before being approached because they realize they've violated their promises. So share these pledges with the coaches and officials in your child's athletic program. They may share your feelings about the need for everyone to agree on appropriate behavior before the season even starts.

One last story. Mike's dad was an alcoholic and abandoned the family when Mike was only two. Mike's mother was manic depressive, undiagnosed throughout most of her life. She and Mike were both victimized by the disease's extremes, alternating highs and lows that resulted in three marriages, three divorces, and frequent descents into a deep hole of promiscuity and alcohol abuse. To escape his mother's unpredictable behavior and to bring more money into their one-room apartment, Mike began working in seventh grade.

Each day he would run out the school doors with his classmates, but then leave them to catch a bus to downtown Chicago, and work six hours selling candy and orange juice in the Shubert Theater. The money helped support him and his mother, but missing homework, strained relationships with schoolmates, and frequent misbehavior in the classroom introduced him almost daily to the business end of his seventh- and eighth-grade teachers' yardsticks.

High school was little different. After-school and summer jobs at Wrigley Field or the steel mills in South Chicago helped buy food, but failing grades, scrapes with the law, continuing turmoil at home, and a subtle, undefined anger made high school a troubled time for Mike. But he discovered football. He joined the team during his sophomore year, quit after only a few weeks, but—at the request of coaches and friends—went out again during his junior year.

Mike became a high school All-American and thanks to some good scores on his college admissions test, received a scholarship to play for a major university. But because of his unresolved problems, within months he was expelled from college for fighting. Eventually he joined the Coast Guard Reserves where he continued playing football. Shortly after discharge, he was offered another scholarship to play football, returned to college, and met one of the most profound influences on his life.

Coach George Kelly, only ten years older than Mike, became a strong but gentle hand in Mike's angry and sometimes violent world. Coach Kelly's approach to life defined the "gentle" in gentleman and taught Mike that only the toughest among us are capable of real thoughtfulness and sensitivity. He taught Mike that a sustained focus on the task at hand can "make it happen," not only on the

217

football field, but in the classroom and elsewhere in life.

Coach Kelly's personal influence and his short but powerful philosophy resulted in Mike's graduation from college, a master's degree, a Ph.D., and a lifelong friendship. Two of Mike's daughters played a variety of sports; the third joined him every time she could to watch football on Saturdays and Sundays. His wife of forty-one years helped him write eighteen books and, during visits for Notre Dame football games, enjoyed with him the elegance and charm of Mike's old coach.

Let's Wrap It Up

By now you've probably guessed that I'm Mike. Without the experience of football and the personal influence of George Kelly, I'm not sure what would have happened to me. One of my fondest memories involves a visit from him during one of his many recruiting trips into the Chicago area. I had just completed my Ph.D., and, while nursing a cup of coffee in my office, he smiled. I asked him, "Okay, what are you laughing at?" He smiled again and said, "*Doctor* Koehler—I thought you'd end up in jail."

Coach George Kelly died recently, leaving behind him not the vacuum of his loss but a wellspring of powerful memories for thousands of athletes who, like me, still use them to transform themselves into better people. Elegance, charm, and genuine concern are infectious. With some luck and a smile from heaven, you and your child might find your own Coach George Kelly. Even if your coach falls a little short (not everyone can be a Kelly), you'll find a colleague and a mentor who can transform the world of sport into the exciting and uplifting experience we all want it to be.

Good luck.

ABOUT THE AUTHOR

As a career educator, parent, coach, and athlete, Michael Koehler knows a lot about kids and sports. The grandson of athletic icon Jim Thorpe, Koehler played football at the University of Nebraska under coaching greats Tom Osborne and George Kelly. After being sidelined with an injury, Koehler decided to stay in school and pursue a career in education. Koehler credits that decision to the strong influence of George Kelly, to whom Koehler has dedicated this book.

Koehler has worked as a counselor, English teacher, college professor, and administrator. He coached high school football throughout his academic career, providing hundreds of kids with a positive and meaningful athletic experience.

Koehler has written and spoken widely on high school athletics and has been honored as a Distinguished Alumnus at the University of Nebraska and as a member of the United States Olympic Committee's Project Gold. This is Koehler's 17th book, following Coaching Character at Home: Strategies for Raising Responsible Teens (Sorin Books 2002). Koehler lives in Northern Wisconsin (Minoqua).

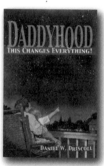